Katy Perry

by Anne K. Brown

LUCENT BOOKS

A part of Gale, Cengage Learning

GALE
CENGAGE Learning™

Detroit • New York • San Francisco • New Haven, Conn • Waterville, Maine • London

© 2011 Gale, Cengage Learning

LIBRARY OF CONGRESS CATALOGING-IN-PUBLICATION DATA

Brown, Anne K., 1962-
  Katy Perry / by Anne K. Brown.
    p. cm. -- (People in the news)
  Includes bibliographical references and index.
  ISBN 978-1-4205-0609-9 (hardcover)
  1. Perry, Katy--Juvenile literature. 2. Singers--United States--Biography.
I. Title.
  ML3930.P455B76 2011
  782.42164092--dc22
  [B]
                                                        2011005969

Lucent Books
27500 Drake Rd.
Farmington Hills, MI 48331

ISBN-13: 978-1-4205-0609-9
ISBN-10: 1-4205-0609-9

Printed in the United States of America
1 2 3 4 5 6 7 15 14 13 12 11

Printed by Bang Printing, Brainerd, MN, 1st Ptg., 05/2011

Contents

Fame and celebrity are alluring. People are drawn to those who walk in fame's spotlight, whether they are known for great accomplishments or for notorious deeds. The lives of the famous pique public interest and attract attention, perhaps because their experiences seem in some ways so different from, yet in other ways so similar to, our own.

Newspapers, magazines, and television regularly capitalize on this fascination with celebrity by running profiles of famous people. For example, television programs such as *Entertainment Tonight* devote all of their programming to stories about entertainment and entertainers. Magazines such as *People* fill their pages with stories of the private lives of famous people. Even newspapers, newsmagazines, and television news frequently delve into the lives of well-known personalities. Despite the number of articles and programs, few provide more than a superficial glimpse at their subjects.

Lucent's People in the News series offers young readers a deeper look into the lives of today's newsmakers, the influences that have shaped them, and the impact they have had in their fields of endeavor and on other people's lives. The subjects of the series hail from many disciplines and walks of life. They include authors, musicians, athletes, political leaders, entertainers, entrepreneurs, and others who have made a mark on modern life and who, in many cases, will continue to do so for years to come.

These biographies are more than factual chronicles. Each book emphasizes the contributions, accomplishments, or deeds that have brought fame or notoriety to the individual and shows how that person has influenced modern life. Authors portray their subjects in a realistic, unsentimental light. For example, Bill Gates—the cofounder and chief executive officer of the software giant Microsoft—has been instrumental in making personal computers the most vital tool of the modern age. Few dispute his business savvy, his perseverance, or his technical expertise, yet critics say he is ruthless in his dealings with competitors and driven more by his desire to maintain Microsoft's dominance in the computer industry than by an interest in furthering technology.

In these books, young readers will encounter inspiring stories about real people who achieved success despite enormous obstacles. Oprah Winfrey—the most powerful, most watched, and wealthiest woman on television today—spent the first six years of her life in the care of her grandparents while her unwed mother sought work and a better life elsewhere. Her adolescence was colored by rape, pregnancy at age fourteen, and sexual abuse.

Each author documents and supports his or her work with an array of primary and secondary source quotations taken from diaries, letters, speeches, and interviews. All quotes are footnoted to show readers exactly how and where biographers derive their information and provide guidance for further research. The quotations enliven the text by giving readers eyewitness views of the life and accomplishments of each person covered in the People in the News series.

In addition, each book in the series includes photographs, annotated bibliographies, timelines, and comprehensive indexes. For both the casual reader and the student researcher, the People in the News series offers insight into the lives of today's newsmakers—people who shape the way we live, work, and play in the modern age.

A One-of-a-Kind Pop Star

"We don't get it."
"Who's going to buy this?"
"We don't know how to sell this."

Phrases like these were uttered about Katy Perry as she tried to launch her music career. Time and again, she was met with confusion from executives at record companies. Many agreed she had talent, but her style was unlike any act they had seen before. Her songs did not fit neatly into any musical categories. Executives simply did not know what to do with her music or how to sell it to the public. As a result, Perry's career had a number of false starts and stalled opportunities.

Perry knew that other musicians, such as Alanis Morissette and Gwen Stefani, had experienced similar problems. Their music and image did not fit mainstream pop music either. Yet these women did not alter their music or personal style to fit the expectations of record companies. They stayed true to themselves and refused to give up. They pushed themselves to continue working for a record deal until their dreams came true. Inspired by these women, Katy Perry stuck to these principles as she fought for a music career of her own.

From Plain to Pizzazz

Perry grew up in a conservative Christian household where she was not allowed to listen to the kind of music she now creates. Nor was she allowed to wear the kinds of fashions for which she is now famous, or watch the kinds of programs she is now featured on. Though loving and supportive, her community was not made up of the different kinds of people with whom she now regularly interacts. By her own admission, Perry's childhood was sheltered and straitlaced.

Her religious upbringing led her first to Nashville to try her hand in the gospel music industry, then to Los Angeles where she discovered an entirely new world of music and fashion. She experimented with different styles for several years, and after much hard work and some disappointment, eventually evolved into the Katy Perry who is currently selling millions of records, appearing on award shows, and fascinating the public with her fashion sense.

Perry has been accused of many things over the years—of selling out her religious roots in favor of fame; of inventing crazy fashions and writing racy lyrics for attention; and of being the invention of her producers rather than her own self. Reporters and critics have wondered how a teenage gospel musician could evolve into a boundary breaking, teasing pop princess. Meanwhile, she has attracted anger from Christian conservatives and gay and lesbian groups over two of her most controversial songs, "UR So Gay" and "I Kissed a Girl."

Perry argues that she is really being true to her creative instincts and that she is more than just a string of gimmicks. "You can't just change your dress, or just change your hair," she says. "That can't just be the basis of success. It has to spawn from something more powerful. And it has to spawn from talent, you know?"[1] Perry's talent involves her vocal abilities, songwriting, and her ability to develop an outrageous and unique style. Perry is particularly known for taking sweet, feminine, and fun styles to an extreme and provocative place. Indeed, no other artist wears outfits like hers. Some of these include fake food covered in sequins, carnival colors, light-up dresses, or candy-covered clothes. Her fashions sometimes draw criticism, but Perry also has the public wondering what she will be wearing at her next appearance.

Still the Same Girl

Despite Perry's transformation from a quiet gospel singer to a flamboyant pop star, Perry feels she is the same person she has

Katy Perry is known as much for her creative sense of style as she is for her talent as a songwriter and performer.

always been. She says she simply needed time to figure out her true personality. She revealed to an interviewer that she often feels like the same girl who first moved to Los Angeles. "I think I'm not exactly what I was born into, but I still have my roots,"[2] she says.

With her career still in its early stages, Perry has many opportunities before her. She has already found success with two albums and is in demand for concerts and television appearances. She has been nominated for and received several music awards. She has married British actor Russell Brand, who keeps her laughing as they travel to one exotic locale after another. In more ways than one, Perry's life already seems to be a teenage dream come true.

Chapter 1

A Clean and Quiet Life

Santa Barbara, California, fits the West Coast's picture-perfect image. The Pacific Ocean rolls to the west, hemmed by seemingly endless miles of sandy beaches. The Santa Ynez Mountains lie to the east, providing a beautiful backdrop to the city's palm trees and gentle hills. Santa Barbara is praised as one of California's most beautiful cities, leaving little wonder that it is the place where Katy Perry feels most at home.

Katy Perry was born in Santa Barbara on October 25, 1984. Her full birth name was Katheryn Elizabeth Hudson. Her mother and father, Keith and Mary Hudson, were both Christian ministers who carried their religion into every aspect of family life. Katy, along with her older sister, Angela, and younger brother, David, went to church several times a week and attended the Christian school affiliated with their Evangelical church. In summer, they attended Christian camp.

Matters of religion were never open to debate in Katy's family. As Evangelical Christians, her parents believed they were following the only correct religion and the only one that would lead them to heaven. According to Katy's parents and their church, followers of other religions were on the wrong path and would not be accepted into heaven.

Katy's community was strict about living a clean lifestyle. Children were allowed to listen only to Christian music, never rock or pop. Their movie choices were limited to films that reflected family values—no swearing, sex, or violence. Her family even had their own name for deviled eggs; in the Hudson household, they were known as "angeled eggs." As a child, Katy accepted these rules and views easily, since everyone in her world shared her family's beliefs. Katy recalls, "Everyone related to me [or] in my circle was from church: church friends, church school, church activities. All my friends weren't allowed to watch MTV or go to PG-13 movies or listen to the radio, so I didn't really know anything different. That's how I was raised."[3]

Perry's parents, Mary Hudson, left, and Keith Hudson, right, raised their children in a strict Evangelical Christian household, where the influence of music, movies, and other aspects of pop culture was very limited.

Evangelical Christians

A number of Christian denominations, including the Evangelical faith that Katy Perry was raised in, exist in the United States. These include Catholic, Lutheran, and Episcopalian. Each denomination varies in its beliefs and practices. Some consider the Bible as a source of wisdom and inspiration, while others believe it must be obeyed word for word—not simply for the spirit of its messages, but precisely as it is written.

Evangelical Christianity exists in many different forms and varies from one church to the next. It is usually distinguished from other Christian denominations by its requirement of members to spread God's message throughout the world. Evangelicals will often approach friends, coworkers, or strangers to talk to them about God and invite them to worship services. They are also known for taking the Bible literally. Whereas some Christians consider certain Bible passages to be stories for the purpose of a lesson, many Evangelicals believe instead that those events happened exactly as written.

Like Katy Perry's family, many Evangelical Christians take a conservative approach to life. They may limit their exposure to certain types of books, movies, and music and restrict their interaction with certain groups of people who do not share their beliefs.

Katy Finds Music and Dance

When Katy was nine years old, she began to sing in the church choir, as did many of her friends. She showed a great interest and talent in music and took voice lessons from several different teachers. For her thirteenth birthday, she received her first guitar—in a shade of royal blue that she chose herself—as a gift from the church. She continued to sing at church until she was sixteen years old.

Dance also became a hobby of Katy's. She took dance lessons at the Santa Barbara recreation center, where she learned jitterbug, lindy hop, and swing dancing—dance styles from the 1920s, 1930s, and 1940s. The instructors and other dancers made an impression on her. "These girls would get out of their old vintage Cadillacs with their pencil skirts and their tight little cardigans and their bullet bras and I thought it was so unique and different than what was going on in the 2000s,"[4] Katy remembers.

Forbidden Culture

Despite her parents' efforts to shelter their children from inappropriate pop culture, Katy sometimes discovered music that was beyond her approved boundaries. She recalls one musical influence that did not win approval from the adults in her life: "There was Alanis Morissette. [The album] *Jagged Little Pill* was huge for me. One of the vivid memories of my childhood is swinging on the swing set singing 'Ironic' at the top of my lungs. I went to Christian school, so I got into a little trouble for that one."[5]

Another of Katy's musical influences was Freddie Mercury, lead singer of the rock band Queen. The band enjoyed popularity in the 1970s and 1980s. Although Mercury passed away in 1991 when Katy was only seven years old, his music had a permanent impact on her. She explains:

> He was a turning point. I wasn't allowed to listen to secular music when I was [a] kid, but there was a time when I was hanging out at my friend's house. We're trying on all our outfits, like girls do, and out of nowhere I heard the lyrics to "Killer Queen." Time stood still. The music was totally different from anything I'd heard. I still love Freddie Mercury. He was flamboyant with a twist of the operatic.[6]

Other glimpses of the world outside Katy's sanitized home life came during a few trips to Manhattan to visit her uncle. Frank Perry was a movie director who worked on about twenty films during his career. His most famous production was *Mommie Dearest*, a biography of film legend Joan Crawford. Katy relates one of her most vivid memories of those visits: "We would go

*Canadian singer Alanis Morissette performs in concert to support her breakthrough album, **Jagged Little Pill**, in 1995. Perry cites Morissette as an early influence on her musical tastes.*

to my uncle's apartment and see the drag queens [men dressed as women] in his neighborhood. That's New York to me. . . . If I wasn't a straight little girl from Santa Barbara, California, I'd be a drag queen in New York."[7]

Fashionista Meets Tomboy

Like many young girls, Katy loved to play dress up and showed a taste for fashion from a young age. "I was always into dressing up, even when I was a little girl," she remembers. "My mom says I would wear a different outfit for breakfast, lunch, and dinner. It was my way of saying I wanted to arrive."[8]

Yet Katy also displayed a strong tomboy tendency. She took up skateboarding when she was thirteen years old, and for a while did not mind a few scrapes and bruises. "As soon as Santa Barbara got a skate park, I was there after school every day,"[9] she says. Eventually, she abandoned skateboarding for safer hobbies, as she explains: "A friend of mine . . . was so good that she ended up going pro. I wasn't quite so good, but I could easily handle a half-pipe, where you're skateboarding almost vertically. I gave it up because I was scuffing my knees too much and I didn't like the idea of breaking bones."[10]

A Short High School Career

After graduating from her Christian school, Katy attended Dos Pueblos High School in nearby Goleta, California. During the first semester of her freshman year, she decided to drop out of school and pursue a music career. Rather than remain labeled as a high school dropout for the rest of her life, Katy passed her General Educational Development (GED) test. This gave her the equivalent of a high school diploma without attending high school.

Around the same time, Katy began to rebel against her carefully controlled Christian upbringing. She started drinking, and before long, threatened to spiral out of control. "I started spending Sunday mornings crying and hung over," she says. "Because crying is what you do when you're hung over."[11]

During this time, Katy learned some surprising details about her parents' backgrounds. Her mother and father had not always lived the clean lifestyle that she had been brought up to respect. Both had gone through wild phases of their own when they were younger. For example, her father had used and sold

Perry's father, Keith Hudson, left, revealed to his daughter his own experiences with drugs and other dangerous behaviors as a young man when she began drinking and rebelling against her parents' strict rules as a teen. Hudson credits his faith with putting him on track to a healthy lifestyle.

Freddie Mercury

Chief among Katy Perry's musical role models was Freddie Mercury, whose life had an exotic beginning. He was born on September 5, 1946, on the island of Zanzibar. His parents were of Persian descent, and his birth name was Farrokh Bulsara. He was sent to boarding school in India from 1955 to 1963. His family then moved to England. Farrokh, who began calling himself Freddie as a teenager, graduated from the Ealing College of Art in 1969.

In 1970, Mercury became lead singer of a band called Smile, and he changed the band's name to Queen. At the same time, he changed his name to Freddie Mercury. Queen's big break came in 1974 when the album *Sheer Heart Attack* was released. The album includes the song "Killer Queen," which was a major hit. A year later, the song "Bohemian Rhapsody" brought more fame to the group and marked the peak of its popularity. Queen and Freddie Mercury brought a unique sound to the music world. The group's songs had the feel of rock music but incorporated elements of orchestra and opera.

Around 1987, Mercury informed his bandmates that he was ill with AIDS. His health declined, but he helped his band record one last album before his death in 1991.

Freddie Mercury, lead singer of the British rock group Queen, is one of Perry's music idols.

hard drugs. Katy's father told her about his mistakes to show her she could escape making similar ones. Both her parents had found God at a time when they were taking part in dangerous behaviors. Katy learned that finding God probably saved her father from dying of a drug overdose, and this discovery allowed her parents to settle into a healthy, cleaner lifestyle. "They needed to find God . . . God found them, really,"[12] she says of her parents' transformation.

Ready for Takeoff via Nashville

Katy's love of music helped her to focus. Her parents knew some people in the gospel music industry, and she took advantage of those connections to meet people and look for auditions. When she was fifteen, she caught the attention of a group of musicians from Nashville, Tennessee, who asked her to visit them and learn more about songwriting and recording. She spent about a year traveling back and forth from Nashville to Santa Barbara. "That's when I started recording and meeting people and learned how to write a song, craft it, play my guitar better. It was like my school of rock,"[13] she says. She signed a contract to record an album with Red Hill Records and felt certain that her career was under way.

Life in Nashville was an adjustment for teenage Katy. Nashville is known for its glitzy country music scene and the famous Grand Ole Opry concert hall that has hosted the legends of country music. Katy's time in Nashville, however, was far from glamorous. She was an unknown gospel artist—and she had a lot to learn. That did not scare her, and she worked hard to absorb everything she could from her environment. "I started going to Nashville to record some gospel songs, and to be around amazing country music [veterans] and learn how to craft a song," she says. "I'd actually have to Superglue the tips of my fingers because they hurt so much from playing guitar all day, you know? And from that, I made the best record I could make as a gospel singer at fifteen."[14]

In 2001, when Katy was sixteen years old, her first CD was released. Titled *Katy Hudson*, it was categorized as a Christian/

The sites of Nashville, Tennessee, tout its world-famous music scene, which drew Perry to move there when she was fifteen years old in order to develop her songwriting skills and record her first album.

gospel album. The front cover features an extreme close-up of half of Katy's face; the back cover shows a close-up of Katy's entire face, her hand resting against her cheek. In both photos, Katy's sun-streaked, chin-length, light brown hair is visible, and the most striking elements are her sparkling blue eyes.

The CD features ten songs with names that subtly hint at Christian themes: "Trust in Me," "Piercing," and "Search Me" are among some of the tracks on the album, which also features "Last Call," "Growing Pains," "My Own Monster," "Spit," "Faith Won't Fail," "Naturally," and "When There's Nothing Left." Katy wrote four of the songs and cowrote the other six songs on her album—an unusual accomplishment for a teenage singer.

Katy's album received only a few reviews, but all had positive comments. A review by Russ Breimeier on the website TheFish .com described her style as alternative pop/rock and praised her songwriting ability, especially for someone so young. Breimeier also gave Katy credit for mixing different styles of music as well as producing a sound that was hers alone. Katy's admiration of Freddie Mercury was detectable to Breimeier, who noted, "The award for the most unique track goes to 'Growing Pains,' which has a goofy but artsy feel similar to Queen's 'Bohemian Rhapsody.'" He went on to say: "I hear a remarkable young talent emerging, a gifted songwriter in her own right who will almost certainly go far in this business. That name again is Katy Hudson. Trust me, you'll be hearing it more and more in the next year."[15]

Across the Atlantic Ocean, Katy's CD also received praise. An unnamed reviewer for the British Christian radio website Cross Rhythms remarked, "Katy clearly is a real vocal talent and the breathtaking fact that she's a mere 16 years old suggests a major star in the making."[16]

The Bubble Bursts

Katy's excitement over the release of her CD would not last long. At the end of 2001, her record company, Red Hill Records, went bankrupt and closed permanently. Her album practically vanished. "It reached literally maybe 100 people, and then the label went bankrupt," she says. "It was not like I was [a major Christian/pop star like] Amy Grant or something. So I went back home."[17]

The setback would not be the end of Katy's career; the young musician was not easily deterred. She says, "I was just like, 'OK, well this is over. What do I do now?'"[18] She remembers that one night, she was watching VH1 and Glen Ballard appeared on the screen. Ballard was a music producer and songwriter famous for bringing new artists to popularity. He had launched the career of girl group Wilson Phillips, and his most successful production at that time was Alanis Morissette's album *Jagged Little Pill*. It is the same CD that contains the song "Ironic," which Katy

Producer and songwriter Glen Ballard, holding the Grammys he won for his work on Alanis Morissette's Jagged Little Pill *album in 1996, recognized Perry's potential and invited her to move from Nashville to Los Angeles to work with him.*

Alanis Morissette

Born in Canada on June 1, 1974, Alanis Morissette has earned international fame as an alternative rock star. She released two dance-pop albums in Canada as a teen-ager. Like Katy Perry, she moved to Los Angeles to expand her music career before she turned twenty.

Several years ahead of Perry, Morissette worked with Glen Ballard to produce songs and land a recording con-tract. They had a difficult time finding a record company that would issue her CD. Eventually, Maverick Records took on Morissette and released *Jagged Little Pill*. When the album came out in June 1995, Morissette's team hoped it would sell 250,000 copies. Two months later, however, the album was given a Gold album award after selling 500,000 copies, and a Platinum award for selling 1 million copies. The album sold so fast that it won Gold and Plat-inum awards simultaneously. In July 1998, *Jagged Little Pill* reached Diamond album status (10 million copies sold).

Both Morissette and Perry were raised in strict religious backgrounds but have gained recognition as artists who speak their minds and do not shy away from controversial topics.

had gotten into trouble for singing as a young girl. Under Bal-lard's direction, *Jagged Little Pill* had won Grammy Awards for Best Rock Album and Album of the Year in 1995. Katy recalls she listened to Ballard discuss Morissette's *Jagged Little Pill* "and I was like, 'Well, that's a really good record. She speaks from my perspective. I want to make a record like that!'"[19]

Through some of her contacts in the music business, Katy managed to schedule an interview with Ballard. Upon hearing her sing, Ballard made up his mind almost immediately. He re-calls, "She played the song and it was OK, that's all I need to know." The next day, he phoned Katy, who remembers him saying, "'I want to move you to Los Angeles. I want to help fulfill your dreams.'"[20]

Katy's parents understood her desire for a music career, but they had mixed feelings about a move to Los Angeles at such a young age. They gave Katy permission to move, but not their blessing. At the age of seventeen, with big dreams and her guitar in hand, Katy packed up her car and moved to Los Angeles.

Chapter 2

The Jungles of the Music Industry

Katy's move to Los Angeles marked a brand-new start. Her days as a gospel singer were behind her, and she began trying to figure out who she really was. Away from the influence of her conservative Christian community, she discovered new music, movies, people, fashions, and pop culture every day. As she puts it, "When I started out in my gospel music my perspective then was a bit enclosed and very strict, and everything I had in my life at that time was very church-related. I didn't know there was another world that existed beyond that. So when I left home and saw all of that, it was like, 'Omigosh, I fell down the rabbit hole and there's this whole *Alice in Wonderland* right there!'"[21]

As Katy adjusted to life in Los Angeles and discovered a new sense of freedom, she continued to learn more about herself. She discovered personal tastes in music and fashion that she had never known. She also realized that the rules she had grown up with did not apply to the rest of the world. "Letting go [of my past] was a process," she says. "Meeting gay people, or Jewish people, and realizing that they were fine was a big part of it. Once I stopped being chaperoned, and realized I had a choice in life, I was like, 'Wow, there are a lot of choices.' I began to become a sponge for all that I had missed—the music, the movies. I was as curious as the cat."[22]

Hard Work and Hard Times

In Los Angeles, Katy went straight to work with Glen Ballard. He challenged her to develop her songwriting and performing skills by writing a song every day. He also encouraged her to experiment with different kinds of music and to find her true style. Meanwhile, Katy sang in small clubs to gain exposure.

Ballard tried hard to sign Katy to a number of record companies. For more than a year, he could not persuade anyone to take a chance on her. "We tried so many labels. But you know, it was the same with Alanis: Everybody turned her down," Ballard remembers. "I think Katy was just maybe too ahead of her time."[23]

Around this time, Katy decided to adopt a stage name. She worried the name Katy Hudson might lead people to confuse her with the actress Kate Hudson. For that reason, she adopted the name Katy Perry, borrowing her mother's maiden name as her new last name.

Perry was working hard at her music career and also to make ends meet. Money was tight, and she had to depend on her parents for help. Living in fast-paced Los Angeles, Perry fell into a partying lifestyle and began drinking heavily again. At one point, she realized what she was doing to herself, as she explains: "Drinking became a problem. It got out of control until I said, Ok—back to work."[24] She knew she had to get serious if she wanted to succeed.

Eventually, Ballard's persistence paid off. He landed a record deal for Perry with Island Def Jam Music Group. Her CD was slated for release in 2005. She was still a long way from success, however. "The first time I got signed, they brought me in a room with three other girls they signed at the same time," she relates. "They sat us down and said, 'Maybe *one* of you will ever make a record. One of you will actually take a swing. The other three can go back to middle America and pop out babies.'"[25] Perry took those words as a challenge. She got busy writing, recording, and dreaming of the day her CD would be released.

Another Door Briefly Opens

In 2004, while working toward the release of her own album, a new break came for nineteen-year-old Perry. She was recruited

Perry poses with Lauren Christy, left, one of the members of the songwriting and production team known as The Matrix. A project that Perry did with The Matrix in 2004 was canceled before it was released.

by a production team called The Matrix to perform as part of a new group. The team consisted of Lauren Christy, Graham Edwards, and Scott Spock. This team had written songs for Avril Lavigne and helped launch her career in 2002.

The Matrix's new project was to be an album with Columbia Records featuring Christy, Edwards, Spock, and new talent to round out the band. A newcomer, British singer Adam Longlands, was brought into the group, and Perry was chosen to complete the quintet as lead singer.

The album, to be titled *The Matrix*, was a major investment for the team. The album was produced at great expense, along with music videos. The Matrix production team began a marketing campaign to stir up interest in the upcoming release. Then, only a few weeks before the CD's launch in September 2004, the entire project was canceled.

Perry was disappointed—but also relieved. The flavor of The Matrix did not really fit her own personal tastes. "Thank God that didn't come out, you know?" she said later. "I had this kind of quirky, unique perspective, and they had a very mainstream-pop perspective, which was really cool, too, but I wasn't used to it. We made a record that sonically sounds brilliant but doesn't say much. . . . My own stuff is very heart-on-my-sleeve."[26]

Staying On Track

Perry still had a goal to work toward—the album that was scheduled for 2005 with Island Def Jam. Work continued on the CD, and the pieces seemed to be falling into place. She recorded music videos for the songs "Diamonds" and "Simple." The CD, however, was doomed. Perry got the unexpected bad news that Island Def Jam was canceling her CD. The explanation was that they simply did not know how to market Perry's music and her style.

Perry was stunned by the news and by some reactions to her cancellation. She recalls: "I had someone say to me that 'Psst, you should probably go home, because you're never gonna get signed again. You're pretty much damaged goods. And you should be in the defect aisle at Ross [discount stores].' And I'm 20 at that point. I'm like, 'I'm defect[ive] goods already?'"[27]

Perry's album was not a total loss. Her song "Simple" was picked up for the film *The Sisterhood of the Traveling Pants* and was released on the movie soundtrack album in 2005.

New Challenges, New Disappointments

In 2005, Perry was starting over again. Her first record company had gone bankrupt. Her chance for a solo album with Island Def Jam had been crushed. Even her work with The Matrix had been abruptly discarded. She was still signed with Columbia as part of The Matrix project, so she and her manager, Bradford Cobb, convinced the company to let her record a solo album. Yet Cobb revealed frustration with the entire relationship between Perry and Columbia. "Columbia was never really willing to embrace Katy's vision," he says. "They were not willing to let her drive. Here was this ambitious young woman with a clear picture of who she was and the willingness to work hard, and Columbia just wouldn't put her in the driver's seat."[28]

Work on Perry's album got under way despite differences of opinion. The CD was scheduled to be released in 2006. Then Perry got more bad news. With the CD nearly completed, Columbia decided to cancel her contract and drop the CD. Cobb was shocked by the decision. He says, "Eighty percent of the record was done, and Columbia decided not to finish it and dropped her. We got the masters back and then started looking for a new home."[29] By convincing Columbia to turn over Perry's recordings to her, Cobb planned to offer the songs to other record companies and finally see the CD released.

Perry clearly felt that something was wrong at Columbia. She says: "They dropped me, OneRepublic, and Jonas Brothers in a matter of weeks. But what do you expect? Old guys in suits— they weren't the ones who were going out to the clubs or coming to the shows."[30] Ballard again showed his support for Perry and his distrust of the industry. "Nobody at those labels got what

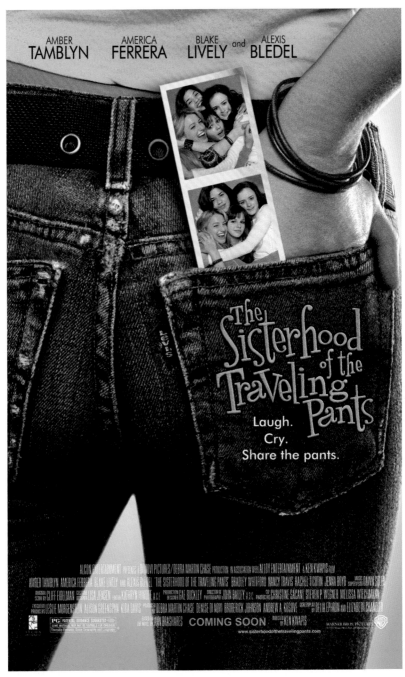

The 2005 film The Sisterhood of the Traveling Pants *featured Perry's song "Simple" on its soundtrack.*

she was about," he says. "She had talent, personality, humor, a sense of fashion. They didn't know what to do with it."[31]

The cancellation was nearly the end of Perry's struggle for a music career. She explains: "My friends were like, 'OK you're delusional.' My parents were like, 'I don't know if this is going to happen for you. We keep putting money into your account for Trader Joe's [grocery store].' It started getting a little bit old."[32]

When Perry had first moved to Los Angeles at age seventeen, she had promised herself that she would keep trying for a music career until she was twenty-five years old. She was twenty-two years old when Columbia dropped her. Time and opportunities were beginning to run out.

Perry's White Knight

Unbeknownst to Perry, she had recently gained an important secret fan in the music industry. Chris Anokute was an Artist and Repertoire executive at Capitol Records. He was young, and he was looking for a brand-new artist whom he could launch completely from scratch.

Anokute had been introduced to Angelica Cob-Baehler, a publicity executive at Columbia Records, at the 2006 Grammy Awards show. Knowing that Columbia was about to drop Perry, Cob-Baehler secretly felt that executives at her company were making a major mistake. She gave Anokute an important tip about the then-unknown artist: "She's a singer-songwriter. She's incredible. She used to be a Christian singer and Columbia doesn't really know what to do with her and they are about to drop her."[33] Anokute asked to get copies of Perry's music and received a DVD and three of Perry's demo CDs.

Anokute recalled his reaction when he first reviewed Perry's work: "It was an independent low budget video of a song called 'Simple'—an early song she did with Glen Ballard. For some reason I thought, oh my God, she is a superstar. She reminded me of Alanis Morissette. I listened to two other songs on the demo. One was 'Waking Up in Vegas' and when I heard that I thought, this is a number one record!"[34]

Gold and Platinum Records

The Recording Industry Association of America (RIAA) represents U.S. artists and record companies. In 1958, it set the standard for the Gold award, a tool that measures the sales and success of a record. A Gold award is presented after an album sells more than five hundred thousand copies.

Due to the growth of the music industry, more awards were created to recognize even greater sales. In 1976, the Platinum award was created to honor album sales of 1 million copies. In 1984, the Multi-Platinum award was established to reward sales of 2 million or more copies.

Katy Perry's album *One of the Boys* has achieved the Platinum award. A number of her singles have reached the Gold, Platinum, and Multi-Platinum levels, with "I Kissed a Girl" and "California Gurls" at three-time Multi-Platinum (3 million copies). Her song "Hot n Cold" leads the way at four-time Multi-Platinum (4 million copies). In January 2011, *Teenage Dream* achieved sales of 1 million copies, earning it a Platinum record.

In 1999, the RIAA again expanded its criteria to recognize sales of 10 million or more albums. Known as the Diamond award, only about one hundred albums have earned this recognition.

Determined to see Perry's career launched, Anokute took the recordings to Jason Flom, his boss at Capitol Records. Anokute did not hold back his enthusiasm. He told Flom, "I've found the next Avril Lavigne meets Alanis Morissette."[35] But Flom was not enthusiastic about Perry and was not convinced that her material and her image would sell. He also knew that Perry had been dropped from two previous record labels. Flom refused to commit to a contract with Perry. Anokute, however, refused to give up. Every week, he visited Flom's office to make his point about Perry. Anokute pleaded with his boss: "Jason, we'll find

Chris Anokute, right, was an Artist and Repertoire executive at Capitol Records who eagerly promoted Perry's work to his label until she was finally offered a contract in 2007.

the record, we'll develop her, we'll figure it out! There is something special about her. I know she is a star. Who cares that she was dropped?"[36]

Something about Perry eventually got through to Flom in early 2007. Anokute remembers the moment: "I don't know what happened but one Sunday almost seven weeks later, Jason emails me, 'It's great, what are we waiting for? Let's sign the girl.' So we . . . offered her a deal."[37]

Still Struggling

Meanwhile, Perry had still been working to find ways to support herself and get her music heard. She seized any opportunity for work and exposure. She sang background vocals in 2006 for the song "Goodbye for Now" by the Christian metal group P.O.D. and later appeared in the music video for the song. She also appeared in a music video with the group Carbon Leaf for their song "Learn to Fly." Her next project was a music video for the song "Cupid's Chokehold" by the band Gym Class Heroes. In the spring of 2007, her work turned a little more girlie—she modeled and appeared in advertisements for Too Faced Cosmetics in the style of a pinup girl.

Life in Los Angeles was not always easy or glamorous. Perry often had to borrow money, and she sometimes bounced checks. Her car was repossessed twice when she could not make the payments for her car loan. She was forced to work at jobs she hated just to pay her rent. One of those jobs was at a company called Taxi Music. She recalls: "I was sitting in a cube, listening to all this horrible music people had sent in and critiquing it, because I was supposed to be helping them get ahead in the music industry. Then Jason Flom called me. That day, I went out for coffee and never went back."[38]

One More Chance

In a brand-new deal set up by Flom, Perry signed a recording contract with Capitol Records. For the fifth time, Perry was poised to record and release an album. In early 2007, the CD that would eventually become *One of the Boys* got under way. Flom met with Lukasz Gottwald, known as Dr. Luke in the music industry. Dr. Luke was a recognized talent as a song-writer, record producer, and music mixer. He had worked with Perry at Columbia, but that album had never been finished. Flom asked Dr. Luke to work with Perry in the studio again. They recorded "I Kissed a Girl" and "Hot n Cold." Perry then worked with songwriter Greg Wells to write "UR So Gay" and "Mannequin." To round out the album, Perry's team selected the best six songs from the tracks she had recorded at Columbia.

To test out public reaction to Perry's music, Capitol Records released "UR So Gay" in November 2007 as an online single. The song caught some attention and sold a few thousand copies. Capitol also shot a low-budget video for the song, which got a great response from fans. Because the single was not a runaway success, however, the executives at Capitol became nervous. Perry's CD seemed like a gamble to them. They were not convinced the album would become a hit.

Meanwhile, Anokute struggled to persuade his company to launch the CD. He looked for a way to prove that Perry's music would be a success. Anokute found a coworker, Dennis Reese, who was also excited about Perry. Reese offered the single "I Kissed a Girl" to a number of radio stations. A Nashville station called The River was the first to take an interest and play the song on the radio on May 6, 2008. After only three days, the station was flooded with phone calls. Listeners could not get enough of Perry's song.

Capitol Records was finally convinced that Perry's CD would sell. On June 17, 2008, *One of the Boys* reached record stores. Anokute felt that their hard work had finally paid off. He explains:

A lot of people think it happened overnight but it didn't.
. . . It took us 14 to 18 month[s] to get her out, develop it and convince people. It wasn't easy to get her signed. I . . . spent a year convincing people. I even had her come to the office, and no matter if it were interns, assistants, media

people, sales people, I would just have her play acoustic guitar and showcase her songs to anyone that would listen. I had nine people standing around in my small office watching her play. This internal buzz building was happening for a year.[39]

Respected producer and songwriter Lukasz "Dr. Luke" Gottwald, left, worked with Perry to record the hits "I Kissed a Girl" and "Hot n Cold" in 2007.

Kate Hudson

After moving to Los Angeles, Katy Hudson thought her name might be confused with actress Kate Hudson. By 2004, she had decided to change her name to avoid identity trouble.

Kate Hudson is a movie actress and dancer who first became popular in the late 1990s. She is the daughter of Goldie Hawn, a former television personality and movie actress who won an Academy Award for Best Supporting Actress for the movie *Cactus Flower* in 1970.

Hudson is known for her bubbly personality, blond all-American-girl looks, and her flawless figure. Her acting talents range from comedy to suspense to dance. She appeared in the movies *The Skeleton Key* in 2005, *Fool's Gold* with Matthew McConaughey in 2008, and in 2009, *Bride Wars* and *Nine*. In 2001, she was nominated for an Academy Award for Best Supporting Actress for the movie *Almost Famous*.

Actress Kate Hudson was already famous when Katy Hudson's career began to take shape, thus prompting the singer to adopt her mother's maiden name, Perry, to avoid confusion.

Sales of the album proved, finally, that Capitol was wise to launch Katy Perry. *One of the Boys* landed on *Billboard* magazine's Top 200 chart, appearing in the number nine position during the first week of its release. Perry was four months away from her twenty-fourth birthday when *One of the Boys* went on sale. She had fulfilled her dream ahead of schedule.

Chapter 3

Katy Perry Makes a Splash

After four false starts with canceled albums, Katy Perry's solo CD finally reached the public. "I Kissed a Girl" was played so often on the radio that Perry quickly became one of the most talked about singers of the summer of 2008. As Perry became recognized for her music, fans and the media also began to notice her fashion style. Perry's approach to fashion gave reporters plenty to talk about.

Walking in a Fashion Wonderland

Perry had been fascinated by the drag queens in New York City during her childhood trips to visit her uncle. Upon arriving in Hollywood, she discovered an endless array of fashions—some good, some bad. In photos of Perry from about 2002 to 2006, her experimentation with style is visible. She can be seen in black rock-star-style leather, grunge outfits with torn jeans and loose tops, satin tops with pants or skirts, bohemian combinations, and denim. She also appeared in outfits that seemed to be her own attempts to break the fashion rules—mixes of denim, florals, lace, leather, and boots. For one publicity photo, she borrowed Madonna's look from the 1980s—a strapless top, fishnet gloves, many long pearl necklaces, a stack of bangle bracelets, and heavy eyeliner. During this time, Perry also experimented with the image of a tough, attitude-wielding rocker chick with spiky hair. In one of her photos, she is seen flashing a switchblade.

Over the years, Perry eventually discovered her true sense of style. Around 2006, her look shifted toward vintage feminine styles from the 1940s and 1950s. She wore dresses more often, especially the type with a fitted bodice and full skirt that was popular in the 1950s. Her color choices also shifted away

Always fashion conscious, Perry experimented with a range of styles in the early 2000s, including grunge and bohemian looks, before settling on her signature pinup image.

from neutrals, black, and denim to bright pastels, jewel tones, and cartoon colors. By 2007, she showed a taste for sequins and anything sparkly.

Fashion critics wondered at Perry's broad range of tastes, especially considering her conservative background. Perry, however, believed that fashion had always been a part of her. She explains:

> From an early age I've always loved the idea of surprising people with my outfits. I change from day to day. On a Monday I could be a Betty Boop figure. On a Tuesday I'll be Uma Thurman in *Pulp Fiction*. On a Wednesday I could be wearing [black] rubber. The next day I'll look like the innocent girl next door. Then there are days when . . . I'll dress normally in jeans and T-shirt. When I pop down [to] the grocery store . . . I leave all my glittery costumes at home. Most of the time I welcome attention, but there are days when I need to keep a healthy distance from it.[40]

Around 2008, Perry's fashion style developed focus. Of all the styles she tested over the years, one look emerged as her favorite. The style that made the biggest impact on her and would come to define her was that of the pinup girl.

Katy Perry—Pinup Style

Pinup girls were young women who posed in cute or provocative poses for photographs to be made into posters and advertising during the 1940s and 1950s. The posters were popular among young men, especially soldiers. As a result, the girls were sometimes photographed in a military or patriotic theme, with flags, uniforms, or other military accessories.

The posters were usually in good taste, with the girls typically wearing bathing suits or shorts or skirts with a cropped top. Their hair and makeup were always perfectly styled. Long, wavy hair, pale skin, and bright red lipstick completed the signature look. The posters were also known for the girls' playful but provocative poses—innocent yet sexy.

Bettie Page—the Ultimate Pinup Girl

Of all the styles Katy Perry has experimented with, the one that has most come to define her is the pinup style. In the 1950s, the phrase "pinup girl" was synonymous with Bettie Page. Page was perhaps the most famous and popular pinup girl of her era, known for her wavy, dark brown hair, red-lipstick smile, and sparkling eyes.

Page had a difficult childhood as a result of her parents' divorce. She and her two sisters spent time in an orphanage while her mother worked two jobs and tried to save money. Young Bettie refused to give in to the difficulty. In high school, she earned a rank at the top of her class. In the 1940s, Page earned a bachelor of arts degree from Peabody College—an unusual accomplishment for a woman at that time. With her husband, she moved to San Francisco and found a job as a model for fur coats.

Page's career quickly took off. In 1955, she was awarded the title "Miss Pinup Girl of the World." Her pictures appeared on posters, playing cards, advertisements, record albums, and other merchandise. As the 1950s drew to a close, Page abruptly vanished from public view. Fans wondered if she had become ill, had died, or had developed mental problems. Page had simply chosen to live a quiet lifestyle and devote herself to God. She died in December 2008.

When Katy Perry discovered the pinup girl look, she was hooked. She integrated the style into her own fashions, makeup, and hairstyles. She changed her hair color from a sun-streaked light brown to a dark chocolate brown, and grew it longer to achieve the curls and waves that defined the pinup girls. Perry also kept her makeup palette very pale, with the exception of bright red lipstick. Other celebrities such as Gwen Stefani and Christina Aguilara have also been known to borrow the pinup look.

Perry's clothing stood out as the strongest element of her pinup style. In many of her concerts and public appearances, she chose outfits inspired by the styles of the 1950s. If any doubt remained about her love of pinup girl style, however, her CD covers erased any questions.

The cover of Perry's CD *One of the Boys* shows her reclining on a lounge chair, with a fringed pink blanket draping the chair. Perry wears high-waisted blue shorts with two rows of white buttons and a 1950s-style bikini top in red and white. A wide-brimmed blue sun hat, red sandals, and red-and-white bangle bracelets complete the look. Perry's lounge chair lies in an idealized backyard with a white picket fence, thick green lawn, numerous colorful flowers, and a plastic pink flamingo lawn ornament. A 1950s pink record player stands nearby to complete the image of fun in the sun. As Perry leans back on the lounge chair, she tilts her sunglasses teasingly.

The interior of the CD booklet continues Perry's pinup theme. Two more photos show her relaxing as if on a summer afternoon—on a lounge chair and in a kiddie pool. The back cover of the booklet features a close-up photo of Perry in a 1950s-style blouse with plastic cherries in her hair. The pose is similar to photos of Bettie Page, one of the most popular pinup girls of the 1950s and one of Perry's idols.

The CD booklet had been carefully planned. Perry and her team knew that Perry's image, as well as her music, would affect the rest of her career. Since her goal was to become a pop princess, she chose a style that she loved and that would allow her to explore her creativity. The result was a girlie, polished look that incorporated humor and sass and allowed Perry to play an innocent and playful flirt.

Her CD *One of the Boys* marked the beginning of a trend in Perry's style. Many of her outfits began to feature artificial fruit as props, jewelry, and costume elements. One of her most famous fruity appearances was at the 2009 Grammy Awards show, where she performed in a dress decorated with sequined artificial fruit. She earned comparisons with Carmen Miranda, the singer from the 1940s and 1950s who wore exotic costumes

Perry struts on the Grammy stage in 2009 wearing a costume adorned with sequined artificial fruit, reflecting the sense of fun and surprise she brings to her personal style.

and elaborate headpieces that included huge flowers, baskets of fruit, and entire bunches of bananas. Perry says:

> I've always been obsessed with fruit, so a lot of my costumes have featured things like strawberry hair clips and watermelon earrings. More recently I've started to incorporate real food into my outfits. At the Japanese MTV Video Awards I wore a leotard embroidered with pieces of sushi. People either look at me and share my enjoyment or else they vote for me in Worst Dressed Women lists.[41]

Perry's unique look drew attention and blended perfectly with her musical style. The complete Katy Perry package fueled headlines and news reports all across the country. Not only had her CD been launched, her career had been launched, too.

From Unknown to In Demand

The entertainment business was also taking notice of newcomer Katy Perry. Almost out of nowhere, her schedule began to fill rapidly with projects and appearances. She filmed an episode of the cable TV series *Wildfire* in which she portrayed a club singer. Singing her own song on the show helped to stir interest in her music. Perry also appeared on an episode of the daytime drama *The Young and the Restless*. The program often featured new artists as a way of giving them exposure. Perry's appearance fell on June 12, 2008, less than a week before the release of her CD. In the episode, Perry played herself. The scene depicted Perry posing for a photo shoot for a fictitious magazine. The glamour of the scene appealed to her girlie side.

Perry's music was also suddenly in demand. Her song "Fingerprints" was picked up to be part of the soundtrack for the 2008 movie *Baby Mama*. The group 3OH!3 asked Perry to share vocals in their new song called "Starstrukk."

Joins the Vans Warped Tour

One of Perry's steps on her journey to break out on the music scene was her appearance on the 2008 Vans Warped Tour. She

Perry performs onstage during the San Diego stop of the Vans Warped Tour in 2008. Her participation on the tour, which typically featured punk, hip-hop, and heavy metal bands, was a surprise to some fans and critics.

had been invited on the tour the previous fall, while production on her album was still under way. A nationwide marathon, the Warped Tour for 2008 consisted of forty-seven concerts sponsored by the shoe manufacturer Vans. Musical acts were accompanied in almost every city by an amateur skateboarding competition and a battle-of-the-bands contest for unsigned bands. The tour ran from June 20 to August 17. Perry was up to the challenge and was inspired by one of her idols. She explains: "Warped is going to be grueling and hot, but I'm ready to survive it—even without showers. Gwen Stefani did the tour back in 2000 with No Doubt and she looked fabulous hopping around on stage in her little polka-dotted dresses. I'm so channeling that."[42]

Girlie Katy Perry in her colorful costumes was an unusual addition to the Warped Tour. Since its beginnings in 1995, the tour has typically consisted of rock bands that are on the verge

Gwen Stefani

Katy Perry names singer Gwen Stefani as one of her own fashion idols and a pop music role model. Both show a taste for vintage fashion, makeup, and jewelry, and both are recognized for bold, unique styles. They often blend fun and whimsical elements into their costumes and performances.

Stefani was the lead singer of the band No Doubt throughout its career. In 2002, the band took a break from performing to spend time with family and recharge their creative energy. Since that time, Stefani has produced two solo albums: *Love. Angel. Music. Baby.* in 2004 and *The Sweet Escape* in 2006.

Stefani has long been considered a fashion celebrity as well as a performer. Her fashion choices range from track pants and Doc Marten shoes to super-glamorous designer outfits. She is also known for a variety of themed costumes for her videos and TV appearances. Stefani's signature look is her platinum blond hair, pale complexion, and bright red lipstick. Like Perry, she finds inspiration in the pinup girl look and in old movies

and musicals such as *Rear Window* and *The Sound of Music.* Her own fashion idols are Marilyn Monroe, Grace Kelly, Jean Harlow, and Sophia Loren.

Gwen Stefani, known for her distinctive and daring sense of style both on the stage and off, is one of Perry's fashion and musical idols.

of launching their careers. In the tour's early years, the majority of bands were punk, but hip-hop and heavy metal have been increasingly in abundance. The vast majority of musicians have been male. Fans of the tour are heavily represented by boys and young men with a taste for alternative music and extreme sports.

In 2008 the Warped Tour included Reel Big Fish, 3OH!3, Angels & Airwaves, Motion City Soundtrack, Gym Class Heroes, and others—a total of nearly one hundred bands. The acts were so numerous that they were split among three separate stages. Perry was one of only a few female artists on the tour. The title of her new album seemed to describe her experience on the Warped Tour: *One of the Boys.*

Perry received several good reviews for her performances on the tour. She was credited with high energy and a playful and fun style. Some critics were surprised to discover that Perry was an excellent singer in a live setting. After Perry's performance in Tinley Park, Illinois, for example, reviewer Jennifer Boyer for the website Dead Hub wrote, "She is very playful with her band members and yes people—she CAN sing live! No lip-synching for this chick. She is the real deal. Always entertaining, Katy hardly ever stops dancing around except when she is playing her guitar."[43]

Perry drew good crowds to her performances in most cities. In Cincinnati, however, reviewer Christy Vowels observed that Perry was not welcomed with enthusiasm. She wrote:

> The Cincinnati crowd . . . seemed obviously bored during the singer[']s set. As a water bottle was thrown at the stage, the crowd exploded for the first time since she took the stage hoping to encourage her speedy exit. . . . With response such as this to her live show one has to wonder if it was just poor choice for her to join a tour like the Warped Tour where the bands tend to be less pop oriented.[44]

As many musicians experience, Perry likely learned that not every performance would be a crowd pleaser.

Romance on the Road

The Warped Tour was exhausting and lacked luxuries. Performers lived on tour buses in the heat of summer and rarely

Perry dated singer Travis McCoy, right, while both were part of the Vans Warped Tour in 2008. By the end of the year, however, their relationship was over.

had a day off from performing. During a performance in Maryland, Perry's shoes melted while they were on her feet. Perry told an interviewer that the majority of her dinners consisted of microwaved macaroni and cheese. The presence of her then boyfriend Travis McCoy, however, made the crude living conditions much more bearable for Perry.

At the beginning of the Warped Tour, Perry and McCoy had become a serious couple. McCoy gave Perry a ring with a diamond as a special gift and explained it was a promise ring—a symbol that they were a couple but without the same commitment as an engagement ring. McCoy also wore a promise ring that was silver and had the name "Katy" inscribed on it.

By the end of 2008, however, the relationship between McCoy and Perry had changed completely. The couple announced that they had broken up. Specific reasons were not given publicly, but Perry had sometimes admitted frustration with McCoy's overuse of prescription medicines. After the breakup, Perry showed little sign of disappointment. She continued to make public appearances and greet the world with her usual energy.

The Critics Speak Up

Perry's CD *One of the Boys* reached record stores on June 17, 2008. As she endured the schedule of the Warped Tour, her album was quickly climbing the record charts. In its first week, it sold forty-seven thousand copies and was ranked by *Billboard* magazine as the ninth highest-selling album in the United States.

Travis McCoy

Beginning in 1997, Travis McCoy was lead singer of the band Gym Class Heroes. The group released its first album in 2002. By 2008, it had released four albums. The band became known for its rap and hip-hop blends. It traveled on the Warped Tour in 2003, 2004, 2006, and 2008. The group's most famous song to date is "Cupid's Chokehold," which borrows from the 1979 song "Breakfast in America" by the band Supertramp.

McCoy began dating Katy Perry in 2007. They were a couple while both performed on the Warped Tour in 2008. The pair broke up at the end of 2008. Perry blamed their breakup in part on his abuse of prescription medicines.

By the end of September 2008, the album had sold five hundred thousand copies, earning Perry a Gold record award.

High record sales are always a sign of success for a musician, but acceptance often depends on another aspect of the music business: reviews from music critics. Responses to Perry were mixed. Some critics praised her creativity and unique sound. Her voice and singing style received mostly positive comments. Reviewer Lizzie Ennever of the BBC, for example, gave *One of the Boys* a nod of approval. Ennever wrote:

> She manages to convey her emotions with a pretty varied and impressive vocal range. She's got a sound that's kind of . . . crossed with Avril Lavigne, but there's a modern . . . tinge, which keeps *One Of The Boys* sounding fresh and funky. . . . In general, this record is surprising—and in a good way. . . . She has a wide variety of sounds and it'll be interesting to see where she goes with the follow-up.[45]

Perry's songs and lyrics caused some confusion among other critics, however. Many questioned whether Perry would be able to put out a second album, or if all her creative energy had been used up. Some called "I Kissed a Girl" a novelty song—a song with a catchy melody but silly lyrics without meaning. Others called her lyrics trashy or empty. Some felt that she would never be able to build a career on novelty songs and lyrics that were fluff without deeper meaning. Reviewer Stacey Anderson from *Spin* magazine was one critic with nothing good to say about the album. Anderson gave *One of the Boys* a 3 on a scale of 1 to 10. She wrote that the album had "no discernible message, just a bleating electroclash soundtrack." The reviewer singled out the song "UR So Gay" by describing it as "a brassy, hiccupping beat, it's momentarily novel, but soon the song wears . . . thin."[46] Similarly, reviewer Genevieve Koski gave Perry's album a grade of D–. She complained that the album lacked substance and wrote: "While undeniably catchy, the hyper-produced songs have a familiar radio-ready quality that becomes infuriatingly mind-numbing over time, and Perry's vocals sound like a less-soulful Kelly Clarkson at best, a drunken, spurned sorority girl at worst."[47]

Predictions for Perry were also mixed. Some critics speculated that she would enjoy a long career. One critic at *Billboard* magazine felt that she had produced an entire album of hit songs; a reviewer from the website MusicOMH called her album "sparky and accomplished."[48] Others, however, did not understand the appeal. On the website Bullz-Eye.com, reviewer Jeff Giles dismissed her album as being overstuffed with instrumental pop gimmicks and not enough true writing talent. He wrote: "Her songs are hooky as all get-out, but they're also packed to the

Perry promotes "I Kissed a Girl," a single from One of the Boys, *at a record release party in June 2008. Reviews of the album and its hit song were mixed among critics, but sales and radio airplay were strong.*

gills with clichés, many of them about how she wants to 'break the mold.' . . . This is annoying at first . . . but it ultimately winds up just being boring."[49]

Whether the comments were positive or negative, one thing was clear: Perry had been noticed. As 2008 came to a close, her album and singles were selling at a fast pace. She began to adjust to the idea of being famous, and she started to look forward to the next phases of her life as a musician.

Chapter 4

Riding the Wave

K aty Perry had struggled through difficult days trying to launch her career. As her music grew popular and she attracted fans, she had to adjust to the idea of being famous. She admitted that she needed some time for her success to sink in. "For a while people have been like, 'Do you feel famous yet? Do you feel it?' And at first I was like, 'No! I'm still going home to my house and my little kitten and making my own dinner and whatever,'"[50] she said in 2008. Perry's fame would become a permanent part of her life as her career continued to grow.

Katy Perry Meets the World

After finishing the Warped Tour and breaking up with her boyfriend at the end of 2008, January 2009 brought new opportunities for Perry. Her next major career event was upon her: On January 23, 2009, her worldwide concert tour celebrating her album *One of the Boys* began in Seattle.

Perry's experiences on past tours helped prepare her for a major tour. She knew she had made some mistakes in the past that she wanted to avoid. She recalls one memorable incident in particular:

> There was the Silly String incident. . . . We were doing this show for Garnier Fructis hair-care products, and they've spent like an hour and a half getting my hair just right. So I'm out there . . . with my awesome hair and I have some Silly String. . . . So I point it at the audience and try to spray them. Only instead of spraying it at the audience I had the

can backward and sprayed it all over my awesome hair. Everybody thought that was pretty funny. Except maybe the hair people, I guess.[51]

Perry's new tour, called *Hello Katy*, sold out around the world. It lasted nearly a year and took her across the United States and to various locales in Asia, Europe, and Australia. It began with visits to nine cities on the West Coast and then jumped across the Atlantic Ocean to Germany. The concerts continued in eleven European cities, including London and Paris. In mid-March, she returned to the United States and played in sixteen more cities, beginning in Houston and zigzagging north through the Midwest, east to New York and Washington, DC, and south again to Florida. Late May found her doing four shows in Japan. Then after a trip to the Netherlands, she performed twenty-one more concerts across Europe. Perry was not nearly finished. The tour continued through June, July, and August, traveling back to North America, then on to Australia, and back to Europe and North America. In November, the tour finally concluded with stops in the Philippines and Austria.

From past experiences, Perry knew the concerts would be more work than glamour. "I knew it would be hard work, but it is really a lot of hard work," she says. "Lots of people who have pretty normal jobs have the weekends off, nights off, not for me. I have no weekends, and on top of that you can't get sick, you're going to all kinds of different countries." Despite the challenges, Perry was grateful for her opportunities, as she explains: "There's no complaining ever, I'm not complaining at all. . . . I know there are, like, 500 girls behind me that want it more than I do or as much as I do."[52]

Reviews of the concerts were generally good. British reviewer Alice Fisher from the newspaper the *Observer* credited Perry's

Perry performs onstage in January 2009 in the early weeks of her Hello Katy *tour to support* One of the Boys. *She spent nearly a year on the road, visiting cities across the United States, as well as Asia, Europe, and Australia.*

A Secret Hobby

Katy Perry has a hobby that few people know about: rummaging for secondhand treasures at garage sales and thrift shops. Considering her taste for vintage clothes and styles, perhaps this love of tag sales is not surprising. As she told an interviewer in 2009:

> From the age of eight, my dad would wake me up early on a Saturday morning and we'd go to garage sales. . . . I'd find a purple glass doorknob from the Twenties and it would be going for a song [that is, very inexpensive]. I have a good eye. I'm not looking to make any huge profits. I'm just drawn to old, well-made stuff that has its own personality. Wherever I am in the world, you can usually find me rummaging through antique shops. Nothing beats the thrill of wandering into a shop in the middle of Australia and picking up the vintage handbag of my dreams for a few dollars.

Quoted in Jon Wilde. "I'm a Natural-Born Glamour Ninja—and I Like It: Katy Perry on Her Unique Style." *Mail Online*, July 21, 2009. www.dailymail.co.uk/home/moslive/article-1198292/Im-natural-born-glamour-ninja--I-like-Katy-Perry.html.

high energy, creativity, and humor, and wrote, "Perry's real magic comes from what so many singers lack: her personality."[53] Perry got especially high marks for her unique ability to surpass typical pop star performers who are often similar and easily forgotten.

By the end of her world tour, Perry's career seemed solid. Her album had received a Platinum record award in February 2009 after selling 1 million copies. Her singles were achieving Multi-Platinum status. Yet she was still considered a new artist, with only one major album to her credit. The time had come for Perry to release another album. Fans, industry observers, and critics all watched to see if her career would explode like a firework or merely fizzle.

The Sophomore Album Test

In the music industry, an artist's second album, commonly called the sophomore album, is considered a test and a turning point. Often, artists release a first album that has great success. Their combination of talent, song choices, and image make a positive impact on the public. The true test of a musician's talent and potential, however, is often measured by their second album. In some cases, the second album marks the end of a career because it does not live up to the creativity of the first album. Sometimes, an appearance in a popular movie or a reality TV show drives sales of the first album, but the artist's talent is limited and does not support another album, such as with singer Bianca Ryan from *America's Got Talent*. In other cases, a follow-up album sells poorly because it comes too long after the first album, and fans forget about an artist or their interests change, as in the case of Ashley Tisdale. The challenge of a second album is to create a CD that is better than the first and to show that the first album had not simply been a stroke of luck.

For her first album, Perry needed to prove to her record company that she could write hit songs and sell CDs. For her second album, she no longer had to prove herself and was free to branch out into different styles and themes. Yet in the background was the pressure that came with a second album. Perry and her team knew that her sophomore album needed to exceed the quality of *One of the Boys* and also make a new statement about Perry and her talent.

Chris Anokute was again Perry's representative at Capitol Records. He carefully considered the direction of Perry's new album. Anokute recalls:

> We wanted to try something different, more rhythmic on the dance floor without losing who Katy Perry was. So I introduced her to new producers like Tricky Stewart, Stargate and Rodney Jerkins. It was cool for her because she'd never worked with an urban producer. But I thought it would give her a different kind of edge, especially since she's a singer songwriter who brings the main ideas to the table when collaborating with producers.[54]

Perry attends the Grammy Awards in January 2010 after wrapping up her world tour to support her hit album One of the Boys. *As she began work on her follow-up album, critics and fans wondered if she could sustain her success.*

Anokute wanted to make sure that Perry continued to grow as an artist. He knew that she needed to sound a bit more mature in order to be taken seriously. By arranging collaborations with new artists and producers of varying tastes and styles, Perry learned how to integrate new sounds and techniques. As she expanded her musical skills and depth, she learned to demonstrate a solid foundation and stretch her creativity.

Perry knew she wanted her second album to get people out of their seats. "When I was touring, I wanted people to dance more. So I wrote an album that made people move, yet didn't sacrifice the story substance that I had on the last record,"[55] she says. In a video on her own website, Perry describes her different visions for the two albums and explains that she tried to make the second album more mature than the first. "The last record to me was a little bit more Betty Boop," she says. "It was very cutesy. And this record is a little bit more Bettie Page. . . . So it's a bit sexier. . . . It's still colorful but in a different way. And it's funny—on the first record I had this obsession with, like, fruit and now it's turned into, like candy and like baked goods."[56]

Saving the Best for Last

Perry's biggest hits on the album, "Teenage Dream" and "California Gurls," were the last songs to be added to the record. Anokute remembers the birth of Perry's idea for "California Gurls." Although her album was nearly finished, she sent him a late-night text message insisting that she needed to write one more song. After thinking about the song "Empire State of Mind" by Jay-Z and Alicia Keys, which praised New York City, Perry was inspired to write a song about California.

Anokute continues the story: "I heard the demo and I was floored. She had a vision for Snoop [Dogg] to guest on the record. I was close to his camp, so I contacted his manager Ted Chung that same day and [said], 'I got a smash for Snoop [and] Katy Perry. It's called 'California Gurls' and it will bring him back to Top 40 radio."[57]

On his next visit to Los Angeles, Snoop Dogg listened to the song and recorded his contributions to the record. Anokute says

Perry performs at the 2010 MTV Movie Awards with rapper Snoop Dogg, who had previously joined Perry in the studio to make a guest appearance on her hit song "California Gurls."

Snoop Dogg

The rapper known as Snoop Dogg started his life with a very different name. His parents named him Cordozar Calvin Broadus, but his mother gave him the nickname that would follow him through his life. She joked that he looked like the dog Snoopy from the *Peanuts* cartoon strip.

Snoop Dogg built a career on edgy rap music. He is famous for his braided hairstyles and his invented words, including the "izzle" fragments that he adds to the ends of words. He has made dozens of television appearances, and his music has been featured in many movies, including *Old School* and *Scary Movie*. He has produced a number of albums and is well known for his song "Drop It Like It's Hot."

Snoop Dogg gladly accepted Katy Perry's invitation to contribute to her song "California Gurls." He added his own rap-style commentary to the background of the 2010 song, inserting an edgy flavor to its lively beat.

it was a huge moment: "He listens to 'California Gurls' and then rolls up some magic and 30 minutes later we're listening to 'California Gurls' featuring Snoop!"[58] Anokute gave Perry full credit for the vision of the song and told an interviewer that she had incredible instincts.

The other latecomer to Perry's album was the song "Teenage Dream." She described it as one of her songs in which she pours out all of her feelings. At different times, Perry had expressed how important it was for her to connect with her audience emotionally. This song had an especially strong emotional charge for her, as she explains: "It's about that feeling that I think so many people relate to, when they get to their 20s and 30s and remember being a teenager and putting all or nothing into a relationship, and usually getting hurt, but it was such an amazing feeling—so pure and lovely and raw."[59]

Perry was continuously aware of what was at stake with her second album. Even though she had a strong fan base and had made it past the hurdle of her breakthrough album, she could not afford to be lazy. "How many times do you see people slump on their sophomore record?" she told a reporter for the *Guardian* newspaper. "Nine out of 10."[60] The album was not going to happen all by itself, and Perry knew she could not behave like a diva just yet.

Teenage Dream Set Free

On May 6, 2010, the single "California Gurls" was leaked to radio stations. The next day, it was the number one song in America downloaded from iTunes. "California Gurls" became the theme song of the summer, with its catchy dance beat and lyrics that tapped into a summery pulse. Three months passed before the CD *Teenage Dream* reached record stores. The album went on sale on August 24, 2010. In the first week, it sold 192,000 copies and appeared in the number one position on *Billboard* magazine's Top 200 chart.

Despite its impressive sales, reviews of *Teenage Dream*, like the ones for *One of the Boys*, were mixed. Reviewer Kitty Empire from the British publication the *Observer* thought Perry's songs lacked the wit and humor of her first album, and that some of the songs, such as "E.T.," did not match Perry's image. She also complained that Perry's attempt at meaningful lyrics was merely a string of clichés. Empire noted, "Perry's second album is a hard-nosed pop product with little of the humour or wit expressed so fluently by her wardrobe," and she referred to "California Gurls" as "pretty lame."[61] Chris Richards of the *Washington Post* could not deny the appeal and catchiness of "California Gurls" but dismissed her other songs as weak, writing that "the hooks are consistently grabby, but even Perry's catchiest refrains quickly start to chafe if you actually pay attention to the words."[62]

The *Los Angeles Times* gave Perry credit for creativity and building an image. It also praised her ability to succeed in different musical styles. The paper's review complained, though, that the CD seemed focused on consumerism and was designed

Perry adopts a California look at a party to promote her album Teenage Dream *in June 2010.*

Recording Studio Secrets

Perry once shared a secret about her recording style with an interviewer. "One of the unique things about me recording is that I like to put down the vocal track with all the lights off in the studio. If I remember the lyrics, I don't want anything to get in the way. I want to be a voice in the darkness." Although Perry enjoys studio sessions because she can take her time with the music, she prefers to play live because of the chance it offers to interact with the audience and feed off of their energy.

Quoted in Mike Burr. "Katy Perry Interview, Bathing Suits, Guyliner, and Mercury Worship." *Prefix*, February 6, 2008. www.prefixmag.com/features/katy-perry/interview/17027.

more like a series of advertisements than a truly artistic album. Rob Sheffield of *Rolling Stone* magazine, on the other hand, gave the album credit for clever songwriting and called it a winner. He wrote, "It's miles ahead of Perry's breakthrough disc, *One of the Boys*, with . . . clever songwriting."[63]

Some of the most positive responses to Perry's album came in reaction to her song "Firework." The lyrics were recognized as speaking to anyone who feels down on their luck or in a bad situation. The chorus pushes the listener to keep trying, break free of problems, and make an impact in the world. The song was praised for its encouraging message and became a frequent request in Perry's public appearances. "Firework" became an anthem for perseverance and hard work on many television shows; in January 2011, the song was played during the *Miss America Pageant* to accompany introductions of past Miss America winners.

Sharing the Fireworks

As Katy Perry gained confidence in her status as a performer, she found new ways to embrace her fame. She discovered that she had opportunities both to give back to her fans and use her talents to benefit others.

Inspired by her own song, Perry launched a "Firework" contest on her website in 2010. She asked fans to tell about someone in their lives whom they considered a firework—a person who was inspirational or influential. Fans were asked to record a video and post it to YouTube. Six entries were selected as finalists, and the videos were posted to Perry's website. In January 2011, college student Cory Woodard, of Georgia, was named the grand prize winner. He named his mother as his firework for always inspiring and encouraging him even though he was confined to a wheelchair. He was awarded a trip along with three guests to one of Perry's future concerts in London. The contest generated many uplifting stories and brought a new depth to Perry's site.

As part of an effort to raise money for breast cancer awareness, Perry found a characteristically unique way to support the Keep A Breast Foundation in late 2008. Along with a handful of other celebrities, Perry allowed a plaster cast to be made of her chest, which involved smearing herself with plaster and allowing it to dry. The hardened plaster was peeled away, resulting in a model of her chest. The model was decorated artistically and then sold at auction, raising approximately thirty-five hundred dollars. Perry was proud of the amount of money earned by her likeness.

Perry took advantage of an opportunity to entertain and honor members of the American military in December 2010. The event was filmed at the Marine Corps Air Station Miramar in San Diego, California. The concert, sponsored by VH1, was called *USO Presents: VH1 Divas Salute the Troops* and included Nicki Minaj, Sugarland, Brandy, and other performers. The lineup included Perry in a tight camouflage minidress performing "Girls Just Wanna Have Fun" with Nicki Minaj and her rendition of "Firework" in a full-length, red sequined gown, as well as two other appearances. Toward the end of the show, she begged her audience, "Be careful out there during the holidays," and understanding their separation from loved ones, added, "I just hope everybody can find a great Christmas

Perry pauses during her performance for **USO Presents:** **VH1 Divas Salute the Troops,** *an event to entertain and honor members of the U.S. military in December 2010.*

and be blessed."[64] Perry received a number of complimentary reviews for her performances.

Several charities have also named Katy Perry as a supporter, including breast cancer awareness, an AIDS initiative concert sponsored by musician Bono, other AIDS groups, and an effort by Gibson Guitars to support Nashville flood relief. She has also appeared in several benefit concerts in the United States, Canada, and Europe. These and other charitable contributions came as a result of Perry's newfound fame. As career opportunities kept pouring in for Perry, she continued to integrate helping others into her hard-earned success.

Chapter 5

The Katy Perry Ripple Effect

After the wide reach and success of the *Hello Katy* tour, by the end of 2009 Perry's music, style, fashions, and controversial lyrics were known worldwide. She had gained thousands of fans but also drew criticism from many sides. In fact, Perry had attracted criticism from the very moment her songs first aired on the radio. Perry's style caused a ripple of controversy that touched on nearly every aspect of her image.

Controversy for *One of the Boys*

Perry's first single, "UR So Gay," immediately drew criticism for making fun of characteristics sometimes associated with gay men. In it, Perry mocks an ex-boyfriend for not eating meat; being pale and skinny; liking fashion, makeup, and classical music; and for acting superior and aloof. Contributor Zack Rosen on the website The New Gay complained, "The song trots out a number of tired gay stereotypes," and "implies an insult. It basically says that the guy in question is less manly for being gay, that he's wimpy."[65] Likewise, popular blogger Duane Moody wrote, "Katy sees being gay as wrong, abnormal, and most importantly, as an insult that she uses to make herself feel better for being dissed." He concluded, "Shame on you Katy Perry. Grow up. Become more than that stereotypical playground bully."[66]

Perry insisted she did not intend to offend gay people or stir up negativity about them. She explained that the song was about someone who took an unusual amount of care with his clothes and appearance—more than a lot of girls. She responded: "The fact of the matter is that we live in a very metrosexual world. You know, a girl might . . . meet a boy, and discover he's more manicured than she is. [She might observe,] is he wearing foundation *and* a bit of bronzer?"[67] Perry said that the point of the song was simply that her ex-boyfriend had all the habits of many gay men—he was well dressed and well groomed—but he was not actually gay. She intended the song to be funny, and she had hoped that listeners would get the joke.

The next single she released was "I Kissed a Girl," which also drew criticism. Controversy over this song ran in several directions at once. First, conservative Christian groups complained

Pastor David Allison noted his dismay over Perry's hit single "I Kissed a Girl" on a sign in front of his church in Blacklick, Ohio, in 2008. Conservative Christian groups criticized the song for promoting homosexuality, while some gay and lesbian groups thought the song made fun of their lifestyles.

A Most Famous Wardrobe

Katy Perry's fashions have become almost as famous as her music. Some of her most creative designs are indicative of her controversial fashion sense:

- Perry wore a dress in a multitude of carnival colors with a three-dimensional carousel skirt at the 2008 MTV Europe Music Awards show.
- For the 2009 Grammy Awards show, Perry wore a dress festooned with artificial fruit and completely covered in sequins. She arrived onstage by riding a giant sparkly gold banana down from the ceiling.
- On May 4, 2010, Perry stepped out in a ruffled pink gown for the Metropolitan Museum of Art Gala. The dress had built-in LED lights that ran the length of the dress.
- Perry opened the season of *Saturday Night Live* on September 25, 2010, in a minidress covered in beads resembling candy. She accessorized with red-and-white candy-striped boots.
- A red sequined dress resembling a movie ticket was Perry's choice for the MTV Europe Music Awards show in 2010.
- During her appearance at a Jingle Ball concert in December 2010 Perry wore a three-dimensional snowman dress.

that the song's lyrics encouraged people, particularly teenagers, to experiment with homosexuality, which they considered inappropriate, even immoral. Pastor David Allison of Blacklick, Ohio, was one such person. In his opinion, "If anyone's seen the video and understands how lewd and suggestive the video is for this song, that is not something young people should go toward."[68]

Gay and lesbian groups were also offended by the song, but for two completely different reasons. The more obvious complaint was that they felt Perry was making fun of their lifestyle and even exploiting it to sell records. As reviewer Sal Cinquemani of *Slant* magazine put it, "'I Kissed a Girl' isn't problematic because it promotes homosexuality, but because its appropriation of the gay lifestyle exists for the sole purpose of garnering attention."[69] MSNBC contributor Tony Sclafani was also critical of the song, but for a different reason. He observed that the lyrics implied that gay and lesbian behavior is wrong or immoral. Calling the song "gay unfriendly," Sclafani lamented, "Well, it's official. It's cool to make fun of gay people again."[70]

Perry thought the debate over her song was silly. "It's just an innocent kiss!" she said. "You know, girls are at a slumber party and they are hanging out with other girls, we're all deathly afraid of that first kiss by that boy who we know is just gonna slobber all over our face."[71] Many interviewers asked whether she had ever kissed a girl, and a few seemed determined to trap Perry into either admitting she was a lesbian or into making an anti-lesbian remark. Each time, though, without hesitation or regret, she answered yes—she had kissed a girl not just once, but a number of times. As for whether she had enjoyed it, she told news anchor Katie Couric, "Well, yeah. I guess I would have stopped after the first one."[72] Perry's honest and lighthearted response to the issue eventually caused the media to lose interest in the topic.

The Controversy Continues

Controversy over other songs on Perry's album soon followed. Much of her music was deemed inappropriate for children and teens, such as the song "Waking Up in Vegas," which describes underage drinking and the use of a fake I.D. Detractors also complained that Perry's songs contained too many references to sexual activity. As a result, her music has been banned by some parents and educators and has been refused play at middle school dances at Catholic schools in the Milwaukee and Denver metro areas and in other parts of the country. A Catholic school principal in Monument, Colorado, stated, "I would never allow Katy Perry's music to be played in our school. It's just too racy and not appropriate for this environment."[73] While many radio stations did not find Perry's lyrics inappropriate, others were pressured by listeners not to play her songs. Indeed, several stations, especially those that play Christian music, refused to play Perry's CD.

Perry explained that all of her songs result from following her creative energy. Her intention was not to lead fans into danger or get them in trouble. She says:

> The way my mind works is not the normal, vanilla, bland idea. I've always been kind of unfiltered my whole life, not only in my songwriting but my friendships, my relationships. I think I just kind of say things, sometimes, that people have thought but never really had the [nerve] to say. . . . Being a songwriter, you've got to tell good stories, and I tell all the colors of the rainbow, not just the pink ones.[74]

Teenage Dream—Not Appropriate for Teens?

Like *One of the Boys*, *Teenage Dream* was met with controversy. The CD earned a Parental Advisory for Explicit Content. A few songs contain curse words, and the songs "Teenage Dream" and "Last Friday Night" describe drinking, sex, and other behaviors inappropriate for teenagers. As reviewer Mikael Wood of *Spin* magazine puts it, "*Teenage Dream* won't disappoint parents looking for reasons to worry about their kids." He describes the song "Last Friday Night" as promoting "an evening of nonstop naughtiness."[75]

Following in the footsteps of her CD, Perry's music videos for *Teenage Dream* also took on more mature themes. The video for "California Gurls" features a candy fantasyland much like a children's game. At first glance, it seems attractive to children and teens, but in fact, the video contains lyrics and movements that are not appropriate for children. In one memorable scene, Perry wears a bikini top with a pair of built-in spray cans that

Perry holds a lollypop stage prop, extending Teenage Dream's *candy-and-sweets motif, during a performance on NBC's* Today *in August 2010.*

shoot whipped cream. The video received positive reactions for its cute, playful elements, but few people missed its obvious sexual references. The "Teenage Dream" video also stirred discussion. The lyrics refer to intense sexual activity, and the video, although filmed without nudity, conveys sexual acts that would earn a movie a rating of at least PG-13. In blogs and on some fan websites, comments ranged from surprise to disgust.

Perry's album cover also drew attention. The front cover portrays Perry completely naked, posing pinup girl–style lying on a cloud of cotton candy. A band of pink cotton candy covers her bottom in order to maintain modesty. The cover image was produced from an enormous painting by New York artist Will Cotton rather than a photograph. The mature nature of the cover artwork, although attractive and artistically tasteful, communicates that the CD is not intended for children or teens, but an older audience.

Inside the CD, Perry poses with more cotton candy. She is also seen in two different crowns made of frosting and candy, and she wears a metallic, pleated dress that resembles a cupcake wrapper. Similar to her first CD, the photos are innocent and playful, yet sexy—enough to make some parents nervous. At least one critic felt that the CD's artwork was simply an effort to sell albums by using sexy images. Tony Sclafani wrote, "Perry's CD cover seems just another in a long line of attention-grabbing tactics by a mainstream pop artist."[76]

Yet despite the fact that *Teenage Dream*'s content was even more racy and explicit than that of *One of the Boys*, overall it received less debate in the media. Possibly, the parental advisory eliminated some debate over it because the CD was clearly identified as being suited for an older audience. Fewer arguments could be made about its appropriateness, given the advisory statement prominently placed on the album's cover.

Perry's Music and Her Christian Parents

A popular topic among reporters, media, and gossip columns was the reaction of Perry's parents to her controversial style and lyrics. Given her parents' conservative Christian background, reporters assumed they would disapprove of their daughter's sexy and outlandish style. Perry insists, however, that her parents are nothing but supportive of her career. As she told Jocelyn Vena of MTV News, "They love and support me. Of course, they have their own opinions, but . . . if they weren't supportive, they wouldn't come to all the shows."[77]

Reporters and tabloids repeatedly hunted for conflict between Perry and her parents, but they never found any. Perry's parents visited her on the Warped Tour in 2008 and watched her concerts. They accepted Perry's relationship with Travis McCoy.

Mary Hudson, left, celebrates with Perry at the release party for One of the Boys *in 2008. Despite the fact that their daughter's revealing fashions and racy lyrics may seem at odds with their conservative Christian lifestyle, Perry's parents have been avid supporters of her career.*

Her father even considered getting a tattoo from McCoy when he found out that the Gym Class Heroes singer was a tattoo artist. Perry noted that her father already had three tattoos that all said "Jesus."

Despite their different tastes, Perry expresses a deep respect for her parents, their religion, and their convictions. She has repeatedly said she has no regrets about her upbringing and is grateful to have a strong foundation to help guide her life. When she struck out on her own, she says she took her values with her. Her parents have never turned their backs on her, even if they disapproved of some of her choices. She explains: "I was respectful of what they wanted while I was under their household, and I took the leap on my own to Los Angeles when I was 17. They love me as their child, but I'm sure they would have had a bit of a different picture that they painted of me. . . . But they totally support me and are just happy that I'm not strung-out and a centerfold."[78]

Anyone hunting for a rift between Perry and her parents likely gave up the search after the video for "Hot n Cold" was released. In the video, Perry portrays a bride at the altar who waits for her fiancé to say "I do." In the front row of the church, playing the parents of the bride, are Perry's own parents. For many observers, this came as a public show of the Hudsons' support for their daughter's career. Questions about Perry's parents settled down after the video was released.

Perry—a Sellout?

Some of Perry's harshest criticism came from the Christian community. Her transformation from gospel singer Katy Hudson to pop sensation Katy Perry had been dramatic. She had shifted from a clean-cut, girl-in-the-next-pew gospel singer to a sassy, flirtatious young woman who did not shy away from curse words, controversy, or cleavage. Reporters and bloggers for Christian publications and websites accused Perry of deliberately choosing controversial themes in order to get attention. They felt she had sold out her true roots in order to gain fame.

An Eye for Detail

Katy Perry has gained wide recognition as an extremely detail-oriented performer who plans each part of her performance down to the smallest element. Her hair and makeup are always perfect. Her performances incorporate the full stage, musicians, dancers, props, and costumes. In an outdoor performance of "Waking Up in Vegas" on the *Today* show in 2009, for example, Perry wore a red sequined minidress with a cascade of fake gems and fuzzy dice. Her band wore suits made entirely of printed fabric that looked like paper money, with black shirts and red sequined bow ties. The stage was decorated with large, inflatable strawberries and bananas, reflecting Perry's beloved fruit theme. Her microphone was covered in silvery crystals with crystal cherries worked into the design. As she told TV journalist Matt Lauer, "I'm a real sucker for a theme. Every day is Halloween for me."

Quoted in NBC. *Today*, July 24, 2009. www.msnbc.msn.com/id/26184891/vp/321232 73#32123273.

Perry performs "Waking Up in Vegas" on NBC's Today *in 2009 wearing a costume adorned with fuzzy dice; her band sports suits that look to be made of money.*

Although her lifestyle has changed considerably from the conservative one in which she was raised, Perry says she had Jesus's name tattooed on her wrist to remind her of her roots.

In some news stories, Perry was described as falling victim to the culture of Hollywood and rock 'n' roll. Reporters liked to point out that Christian performers Amy Grant, Switchfoot, and P.O.D. had crossed into mainstream music without abandoning their religious roots. Perry, on the other hand, was criticized for not maintaining a connection to her faith. As Christian columnist Mike Rimmer of the Christian radio website Cross Rhythms said of Perry: "It seems that she has been willing to make compromises with her image and song content in order to create CD sales and create a notorious image. As I've watched from a distance the choices she's made, I have sometimes been disappointed."[79]

Perry insisted that she had not abandoned her religion or her values. She maintains she still feels a strong connection to God. Her views about religion had changed, but deep down, she said the foundation her parents had laid was still there. She explained: "I'm not exactly the poster child for anything religious, and I'm definitely not what I grew up in. But I got this Jesus tattoo on my wrist when I was 18, because I know that it's always going to be a part of me. When I'm playing, it's staring right back at me, saying, 'Remember where you came from.'"[80]

Perry and Elmo's Play Date Canceled

Controversy over Perry's wardrobe erupted in September 2010 when she was invited to film a segment for *Sesame Street* with Elmo the Muppet. Singers and actors have frequently appeared on *Sesame Street* over the years to teach lessons about counting, colors, or feelings. In Perry's segment, she changed lyrics from her song "Hot n Cold" to teach about opposites. Her lyrics included the line "I wore' dress-up clothes" to indicate her lime-green costume and veiled headpiece. Perry and Elmo played along to the song.

After the segment appeared on YouTube, the producers of *Sesame Street* were flooded with complaints. Parents were upset that Perry's outfit revealed too much cleavage. The neckline was somewhat low cut, and even though Perry's chest was covered by fabric mesh, the costume was thought to be inappropriate for young viewers. The producers had approved the outfit for the filming of the segment, so they were surprised by the reaction.

Not wishing to offend parents, *Sesame Street*'s producers pulled the segment from the show. Perry and Elmo both appeared publicly and said that they understood the problem but were somewhat disappointed. Elmo told *Good Morning America*'s George Stephanopoulos that he looked forward to another visit from Perry. "Elmo loves Miss Katy and we had a good time. So we'll have another play date."[81]

Sesame Street's Elmo filmed a segment with Perry in 2010 that was pulled from the show after parents complained that the singer's costume was too revealing for a children's program.

During the Elmo controversy as well as other criticisms of her style, Perry has remained cool and calm. She has never become publicly angry or lashed out at critics. She has brushed aside criticism and told interviewers that her choices simply reflect her personality. Unlike some celebrities who make remarks they later regret, Perry typically handles her critics with poise and sophistication.

Chapter 6

Better than a Teenage Dream

Katy Perry's successful albums got people talking, and her wardrobe, videos, and style kept them interested. This combination made her irresistible for appearances on television, in movies, on award shows, and in concert. On the heels of her popular albums, Perry was a virtual domino effect of activity, moving from one appearance to another in a seemingly endless stream. Her travel, public appearances, and whirlwind romance throughout 2009 and 2010 must have truly felt like a teenage dream come true.

Movie Turns to Romance

Perry's fame brought her many new experiences, but one particular invitation permanently impacted her life. During the summer of 2009, Perry was invited to make a cameo appearance in the movie *Get Him to the Greek*. She was slated to act in a kissing scene with the movie's star, Russell Brand, who played an out-of-control British rock star preparing to make a comeback. Despite Brand's bad-boy Hollywood reputation, Perry described him as "really gentle in person and just had this vibe about him that was captivating."[82] Both enjoyed the scene and were happy with the results, but it was eventually cut from the movie.

Perry crossed paths with Brand again in September at the MTV 2009 Video Music Awards show at Radio City Music Hall in New York. Perry attended the awards show as a nominee for

Best Female Video for her song "Hot n Cold." Brand was hosting the Video Music Awards for the second year in a row. He made a dramatic, rock-star-style entrance onto the stage amid fireworks and special effects. He was accompanied by Katy Perry and guitarist Joe Perry of Aerosmith. Together, they sang Queen's "We Will Rock You." Brand kept the audience laughing with a stream of jokes sprinkled heavily with curse words.

British comedian Russell Brand, left, escorts Perry to the premiere of Get Him to the Greek in June 2010. The couple first met on the set of the movie, although their scene together did not make the final cut.

Perry described her encounter with Brand as somewhat flirtatious. "I really gave him a run for his money," she told an interviewer for *Seventeen* magazine. "I was just hamming it up with him, and we were very comically competitive, but we also had some nice conversations. He wanted to take me home the night after the VMAs [Video Music Awards]. We were out after the show, and I was like, 'Nuh-uh. I'm not that kind of girl. I need dinner and conversation. I know about you.' So we went out to dinner and I went home."[83]

Soon after, Perry found herself in a predicament. She and a friend had plans to vacation in Thailand, but her friend became sick and had to back out. Brand offered to go on the trip with her. Perry thought the plan was crazy, but they met at the airport and jetted to Thailand together. That trip, which Perry described as their "second date," led to other vacations in Paris and London, and the pair soon revealed they were dating.

When their attraction turned to love, Perry decided to reveal her feelings to Brand in her typically flamboyant way. She hired a skywriter to spell out "I Love You" above his home. The experience turned out to be somewhat nerve-racking for Perry, as she explains: "He hadn't told me he loved me yet, but I was just gonna take a chance because I could feel it. . . . And thank God he told me he loved me that morning. I didn't really even say it back because I wanted to save it. We walked out to the balcony of his house, and I said, 'Look up.'"[84]

An Exotic Proposal

The romance between Perry and Brand continued to sizzle. When Perry told Brand she loved Indian culture, he arranged for them to go to India as a Christmas gift. Together, they enjoyed traditional tourist sites such as the Taj Mahal, and Perry had her hand painted with a henna tattoo. The highlight of the trip was on New Year's Eve in Jaipur, when Brand surprised Perry with an engagement ring. Perry accepted his proposal happily, and the news was made public by their agents on January 6, 2010.

Perry's ring became the focus of great attention. While in Delhi, Brand had secretly met with jewelry designer Hanut

Brand leads Perry out of his London home, where paparazzi await in January 2010. Perry grips Brand's arm with a hand adorned with a new engagement ring, which he had given her the previous New Year's Eve.

Singh, who had been recommended by friends. Singh showed Brand some of his favorite designs as well as a rare Golconda diamond from India—diamonds that have a reputation as the whitest and purest stones in the world. Brand made up his mind easily. A few weeks later, Perry's ring was sought after by photographers after news of the engagement went public.

Waiting for Wedding News

Throughout 2010, Perry's and Brand's public appearances were sweet, authentic, even funny. When asked why Perry was so special on the television show *The View*, for example, Brand said, "As soon as I met her, she was a long way away, maybe like forty yards away, she threw a bottle right across the room and hit me on the head and at first I thought, a woman with an arm like that could be useful in a marriage, for defense purposes." He admitted that his head hurt after getting hit and that people around him laughed, but he was intrigued. He expressed his sentiments about her by saying, "I want to take care of her and I love her."[85]

By May 2010, reports circulated that a Perry-Brand wedding would take place sometime in October. Later news revealed it would be held in India. When the couple was spotted boarding a plane to India on October 20, the entertainment media started scrambling for coverage. Perry, however, begged for privacy on her Twitter page: "Greatest gift u can give us is respect & ♥ during this private X. No use wasting ur X w/ STOLEN or FALSE info. Thnku for this."[86] (Translation: Greatest gift you can give us is respect and love during this private time. No use wasting your time with stolen and false information. Thank you for this.)

A Secret Garden Wedding

A few days later, Perry's and Brand's representatives confirmed that the couple was married on October 23, 2010, in the countryside of northern India. The ceremony was performed by a Christian minister, a longtime friend of Perry's parents. Only invited guests—family and friends—were in attendance. Var-

Russell Brand

In addition to being Katy Perry's husband, Russell Brand is a British actor and comedian. As a performer, he is known for his endless energy and his willingness to try almost anything. In public, his style appears to be a cross between rock star and nineteenth-century poet, blending black jeans, ruffled shirts, brocade jackets, leather, and heavy jewelry. He is also famous for his unruly hair, the wild, unfocused, maniacal gleam in his eyes, and his fondness for curse words. Brand is also known for his battle with drug and alcohol addiction and for dating hundreds of women.

Brand has appeared in several movies. He played Adam Sandler's wacky best friend in the 2008 film *Bedtime Stories*. Also in 2008, he appeared as the character Aldous Snow in the movie *Forgetting Sarah Marshall*, and later played the lead role in the 2010 film *Get Him to the Greek*. Brand and Perry crossed paths a few times but became interested in each other at the MTV 2009 Video Music Awards show. They were married October 23, 2010.

ious reports estimated there were about seventy to one hundred guests.

A number of colorful rumors followed the wedding. One claimed that Brand's wedding gift to his new wife was a tiger. This was false; tigers are protected animals in India and cannot be bought or sold. Some of the gossip also described the wedding festivities as going on for a full week, yet the bride and groom were in the country for only five days.

Accurate details about the wedding trickled forth in the weeks following the ceremony. Brand, Perry, and their guests stayed at a resort near Ranthambore National Park, a wildlife sanctuary known for its tiger population, not far from Jaipur. Guests were treated to traditional Indian music, acrobats and jugglers, and safari trips. On the day of the wedding, the trees lining the entrance to the sanctuary were covered in white lights.

A resort near India's Ranthambore National Park was the site of Perry and Brand's wedding in October 2010. Details of the event were kept secret and held under intense security.

Photos of the bride and groom were absent in the media. Reporters spent a great amount of time guessing the details of the wedding, especially Perry's wedding gown. To the disappointment of fans and the media, the couple never released any wedding photos to the public. Two days after their wedding, Perry and Brand flew to the Maldives for their honeymoon—and to celebrate Perry's twenty-sixth birthday the same day.

In Demand at Award Shows

In addition to enjoying a dreamlike romance and wedding, Perry's dream of becoming an award-winning musician also came true in 2010. That year, she was nominated for a number of awards, including several international recognitions. Perry was also invited to appear as a performer and presenter.

September 2010 brought the first of many appearances for Perry. She attended the MTV Video Music Awards ceremony as a nominee for the second time, with nominations for Best Female Video and Best Pop Video for "California Gurls." In addition to being a nominee, she was paired with singer Nicki Minaj to present the award for Best Male Video to Eminem. In both of Perry's nominated categories, however, Lady Gaga took home the awards.

Perry and Brand finished their honeymoon in time to attend the MTV Europe Music Awards ceremony in Madrid, Spain, on November 7. In their first public appearance since their marriage, the couple was peppered with questions about their wedding and revealed their matching diamond-encrusted wedding bands.

The MTV Europe Music Awards were familiar territory for Perry after hosting the show in 2008 and 2009. For 2010, her duties were lighter. As an example of her popularity, she was nominated in five categories and tied with Lady Gaga for the most nominations of the year.

Perry's performance of the song "Firework" at the MTV Europe Music Awards in November 2010 featured an actual fireworks display.

California Dreams World Tour

Katy Perry crisscrossed the globe on a long concert tour in 2011. The tour started in Lisbon, Portugal, on February 20 and continued throughout Europe until the first week of April. After a break of about two weeks, the tour continued in Australia and New Zealand until May 15. Perry then jetted to Japan for several concerts, finishing around May 24. The tour went through the United Kingdom in October and continued in Europe through the first week of November. Her schedule also included dozens of appearances in the United States.

Perry also had the honor of performing her new single "Firework." In Perry's typically dramatic style, the performance featured six dancers with handheld fireworks, as well as large-scale fireworks that engulfed the entire stage. The evening ended on a high note as Perry took home the award for Best Video.

Perry's dream continued as she attended more award shows, gathered more nominations, and took home a number of awards. The winter award season resulted in a long list of acknowledgments. In August 2010, she won two Teen Choice Awards for Choice Music Single and Choice Summer Music Song ("California Gurls"). In November *Cosmopolitan* magazine honored Perry as part of its Ultimate Women of the Year Awards, where she was named Ultimate International Music Star. Also that month, the American Music Awards featured Perry performing her song "Firework," and she earned three nominations. Perry wrapped up the year with a performance at the Grammy Awards nomination event, where she learned that she was nominated for four Grammy Awards. Her popularity followed her into 2011, which began with Perry winning two People's Choice Awards for Favorite Female Artist and Favorite Internet Sensation.

Perry's whirlwind of appearances included a number of other kinds of shows, too. In May 2009, she was featured on *American Idol* as a performer. She sang "Waking Up in Vegas" while wearing a low-cut white leotard and cape, as a feminine version of Elvis Presley. In January 2010, Perry was invited to serve as a guest judge at auditions for the show's ninth season. She joined the ranks of other guest judges such as Shania Twain, Joe Jonas, and Avril Lavigne. Perry's appearance made waves among *American Idol* fans. She made tough decisions about the hopeful contestants and gave brutally honest critiques that sometimes bordered on harsh. Perry became entangled with fellow judge Kara DioGuardi a number of times. The two women disagreed about many contestants, and Perry showed no hesitation about voicing her disputes with veteran judge DioGuardi. They shared jabs and mild threats with each other, and left viewers shocked and entertained with their catty exchanges. Despite the conflict, Perry appeared calm and confident and seemed to enjoy her experience.

No Time to Slow Down

As the ultimate girlie girl and a former cosmetics model, one of the highlights of Perry's busy year was her performance at the Victoria's Secret Fashion Show. Filmed in New York and broadcast on nationwide television, Perry appeared twice, first singing "Firework" in a purple satin leotard dress with an enormous detachable train. Later, she sang a medley of her hits while wearing a provocatively styled Shirley Temple–type dress with layers of petticoats. Perry clearly enjoyed the event, dancing onstage with the models following the finale. She says, "I was so excited to be a part of that amazing show because it's brilliant, the costumes are beautiful."[87]

If Katy Perry ever dreamed of playing a cartoon character, that wish came true twice in 2010. During the summer, Perry recorded the voice of Smurfette for a new movie version of *The Smurfs*, scheduled for release in August 2011. Perry found her role to be especially funny, since she had not been allowed to watch the cartoon show as a child. "I've never seen an episode

because my parents wouldn't let me," she explains. "My mom thought that Smurfette was [not a good role model]. . . . And now I showed her. I called her up and was like, 'Guess what, Mom: I'm Smurfette!'"[88]

Then in December 2010, Perry was featured in the holiday special for the animated series *The Simpsons*. She played herself in animated scenes and, in a first for the show, played in live action scenes with puppet versions of the Simpson family. Perry's scenes were full of humor. After hugging the puppet version of cranky Mr. Burns and giving him a kiss on the top of his head, Burns quipped, "I kissed a girl and I liked it!"[89]

The Future of Katy Perry

Perry has big plans for her future, which include changing her name to Katy Brand. With two hit records and a worldwide tour on her schedule, Perry seems to be poised for a long and successful career. In interviews, she gives off endless energy and shows unlimited creativity. Fans eagerly await her next concert, next CD, and next outrageous outfit. Critics watch her carefully, wondering if the pop princess can keep her image fresh and original or if she will go stale and become cliché. No matter what happens next, Perry has succeeded in setting off her musical career like a firework. Her life and career seem truly to be a teenage dream.

Introduction: A One-of-a Kind Pop Star

1. Quoted in CBSNews.com. "Katy Perry's Sultry Success." September 26, 2010. www.cbsnews.com/video/watch/?id=6902204n&tag=mncol;lst;4.
2. Quoted in CBSNews.com. "'All Access': Katy Perry." February 4, 2009. www.cbsnews.com/stories/2009/02/04/entertainment/grammy2009/main4775775.shtml.

Chapter 1: A Clean and Quiet Life

3. Quoted in Amy Spencer. "Katy Perry (She Kisses Boys, Too!)." *Glamour,* January 1, 2010. www.glamour.com/magazine/2010/01/katy-perry-she-kisses-boys-too.
4. Quoted in *Seventeen*. "Find Out What Influences Katy Perry's Cute Style!." February 5, 2009. www.seventeen.com/fashion/blog/katy-perry-fashion-qa-interview.
5. Quoted in Mike Burr. "Bathing Suits, Guyliner, and Mercury Worship." *Prefix*, February 6, 2008. www.prefixmag.com/features/katy-perry/interview/17027.
6. Quoted in Burr. "Bathing Suits, Guyliner, and Mercury Worship."
7. Quoted in Rob Sheffield. "Girl on Girl: Katy Perry." *Blender*, September 24, 2008. www.blender.com/guide/61418/girlongirl.html?p=4.
8. Quoted in Sheffield. "Girl on Girl."
9. Quoted in Sheffield. "Girl on Girl."
10. Quoted in Jon Wilde. "I'm a Natural-Born Glamour Ninja—and I Like It: Katy Perry on Her Unique Style." *Mail Online*, July 21, 2009. www.dailymail.co.uk/home/moslive/article-1198292/Im-natural-born-glamour-ninja--I-like-Katy-Perry.html.
11. Quoted in Sheffield. "Girl on Girl."
12. Quoted in CBSNews.com. "'All Access': Katy Perry."

13. Quoted in Leah Greenblatt. "'Girl' on Top." *Entertainment Weekly*, July 25, 2008. www.ew.com/ew/article/0,,20214772,00.html.

14. Quoted in James Montgomery. "Katy Perry Dishes on Her 'Long and Winding Road' from Singing Gospel to Kissing Girls." MTV.com, June 24, 2008. www.mtv.com/news/articles/1589848/20080623/id_1962774.jhtml.

15. Russ Breimeier. "Katy Hudson." Review. *Christianity Today*. www.christianitytoday.com/ct/music/reviews/2001/katyhudson.html.

16. "Review: Hudson, Katy—Katy Hudson." Cross Rhythms, July 26, 2001. www.crossrhythms.co.uk/articles/42/p1.

17. Quoted in Greenblatt. "'Girl' on Top."

18. Quoted in CBSNews.com. "'All Access': Katy Perry."

19. Quoted in CBSNews.com. "'All Access': Katy Perry."

20. Quoted in CBSNews.com. "'All Access': Katy Perry."

Chapter 2: The Jungles of the Music Industry

21. Quoted in Gary Graff. "Interview: Katy Perry—Hot n Bold." *Scotsman* (Edinburgh), February 21, 2009. http://thescotsman.scotsman.com/features/Interview-Katy-Perry-Hot.4988069.jp.

22. Quoted in Mark Moring. "Katy Perry: I'm Still a Christian." *Christianity Today Entertainment*, August 6, 2010. http://blog.christianitytoday.com/ctentertainment/2010/08/katy-perry-im-still-a-christia.html.

23. Quoted in Greenblatt. "'Girl' on Top."

24. Quoted in Sheffield. "Girl on Girl."

25. Quoted in Sheffield. "Girl on Girl."

26. Quoted in Greenblatt. "'Girl' on Top."

27. Quoted in CBSNews.com. "'All Access': Katy Perry."

28. Quoted in Cortney Harding. "Single Lady." *Billboard*, January 31, 2009, p. 22.

29. Quoted in Harding. "Single Lady," p. 22.

30. Quoted in Sheffield. "Girl on Girl."

31. Quoted in Sheffield. "Girl on Girl."

. Quoted in Christina Fuoco-Karasinski. "Perseverance Paying Off for Katy Perry." Live Daily, June 13, 2008. www.live daily.com/archive/news/14375.html.

33. Quoted in Jan Blumentrath. "Interview with Chris Ano-kute." Hit Quarters, October 18, 2010. www.hitquarters .com/index.php3?page=intrview/opar/intrview_Chris_ Anokute_Interview.html.

34. Quoted in Blumentrath. "Interview with Chris Anokute."

35. Quoted in Blumentrath. "Interview with Chris Anokute."

36. Quoted in Blumentrath. "Interview with Chris Anokute."

37. Quoted in Blumentrath. "Interview with Chris Anokute."

38. Quoted in Dave Stone. *Russell Brand & Katy Perry: The Love Story*. London: John Blake, 2010, p. 243.

39. Quoted in Blumentrath. "Interview with Chris Anokute."

Chapter 3: Katy Perry Makes a Splash

40. Quoted in Wilde. "I'm a Natural-Born Glamour Ninja—and I Like It."

41. Quoted in Wilde. "I'm a Natural-Born Glamour Ninja—and I Like It."

42. Quoted in Patrick Luce. "Katy Perry Joins the Vans Warped Tour This Summer." Monsters and Critics, May 29, 2008. www.monstersandcritics.com/music/news/article_ 1408263.php/Katy_Perry_joins_The_Vans_Warped_Tour_ this_summer.

43. Jennifer Boyer. "Katy Perry Holds Her Own on Warped Tour." Dead Hub, August 12, 2008. http://thedeadhub .com/2008/08/12/katy-perry-holds-her-own-on-warped-tour.

44. Christy Vowels. "Warped Tour in Cincinnati, Ohio: Cold Reception for Katy Perry." Associated Content, August 26, 2008. www.associatedcontent.com/article/958849/warped_ tour_in_cincinnati_ohio_cold.html?cat=33.

45. Lizzie Enrever. "Katy Perry *One of the Boys* Review." BBC Music, September 22, 2008. www.bbc.co.uk/music/ reviews/dv25

46. Stacey Anderson. "Katy Perry *One of the Boys*." *Spin*. www .spin.com/reviews/katy-perry-one-boys-capitol.

47. Genevieve Koski. "*One of the Boys.*" *Onion*, July 7, 2008. www.avclub.com/articles/katy-perry-one-of-the-boys,6983.

48. Darren Harvey. "Katy Perry—*One of the Boys.*" MusicOMH, September 15, 2008. www.musicomh.com/albums/katy-perry_0808.htm.

49. Jeff Giles. "Katy Perry: *One of the Boys.*" Bullz-Eye.com. www.bullz-eye.com/cdreviews/giles/katy_perry-one_of_the_boys.htm.

Chapter 4: Riding the Wave

50. Quoted in Greenblatt. "'Girl' on Top."

51. Quoted in Burr. "Katy Perry Interview, Bathing Suits, Guyliner, and Mercury Worship."

52. Quoted in *Sunday Star Times* (Fairfax, New Zealand). "Katy Perry: Girl Trouble." October 24, 2008. www.stuff.co.nz/sunday-star-times/entertainment/more-entertainment-stories/688815.

53. Alice Fisher. "So Much More than the Girl Next Door." *Observer* (London), June 14, 2009. www.guardian.co.uk/music/2009/jun/14/katy-perry-shepherds-bush-review?INTCMP=SRCH.

54. Quoted in Blumentrath. "Interview with Chris Anokute."

55. Quoted in "Katy Perry." Amazon.com. www.amazon.com/Katy-Perry/e/B001IGOIQM/ref=ac_dpt_sa_bio/180-69239 00-9883813.

56. Quoted in "What's Behind Your Visual Transformation for *Teenage Dream*?." Katy Perry—Official Website, November 8, 2010. www.katyperry.com.

57. Quoted in Blumentrath. "Interview with Chris Anokute."

58. Quoted in Blumentrath. "Interview with Chris Anokute."

59. Quoted in Tom Shone. "Katy Perry: You Have to Bust Your Ass at This." *Guardian* (Manchester), August 7, 2010. www.guardian.co.uk/music/2010/aug/07/katy-perry-interview.

60. Quoted in Shone. "Katy Perry."

61. Kitty Empire. "Katy Perry: *Teenage Dream.*" *Observer* (London), August 22, 2010. www.guardian.co.uk/music/2010/aug/22/katy-perry-teenage-dream-review.

62. Chris Richards. "Album Review of *Teenage Dream* by Katy Perry." *Washington Post*, August 24, 2010. www.washington

post.com/wp-dyn/content/article/2010/08/23/AR201008
2304256.html.

63. Rob Sheffield. "Katy Perry *Teenage Dream*." *Rolling Stone*, August 23, 2010. www.rollingstone.com/music/albumreviews/
teenage-dream-20100823.

64. Quoted in Mike Cidoni. "Katy Perry Supreme as 'Divas' Salutes Troops." KATU.com, December 4, 2010. www.katu
.com/news/entertainment/111329749.html.

Chapter 5: The Katy Perry Ripple Effect

65. Zack Rosen. "Music: Katy Perry: The New Gay Interview." New Gay, June 10, 2008. http://thenewgay.net/2008/06/
katy-perry-new-gay-interview.html.

66. Duane Moody. "What Do You Have Against Gay People, Katy Perry?." DuaneMoody.com, June 9, 2008. www.duan
emoody.com/2008/06/what-do-you-have-against-gay-
people-katy-perry.

67. Quoted in Sophie Harris. "Katy Perry on the Risqué Business of 'I Kissed a Girl.'" *Sunday Times* (London), August 30, 2008. http://entertainment.timesonline.co.uk/tol/arts_and_
entertainment/music/article4619220.ece.

68. Quoted in Dan Boniface. "Church's Attack on Pop Culture Leads to Controversy." 9News.com. www.9news.com/news/
watercooler/article.aspx?storyid=99193&catid=337.

69. Sal Cinquemani. "Katy Perry *One of the Boys*." *Slant*, June 15, 2008. www.slantmagazine.com/music/review/katy-perry-
one-of-the-boys/1397.

70. Tony Sclafani. "Media Giving Katy Perry a Pass on 'Kiss.'" *Today* Music, July 22, 2008. http://today.msnbc.msn.com/
id/25802385/ns/today-entertainment.

71. Quoted in Harris. "Katy Perry on the Risqué Business of 'I Kissed a Girl.'"

72. Quoted in CBSNews.com. "'All Access': Katy Perry."

73. Mary Hoffmann. Personal interview. December 30, 2010.

74. Quoted in Graff. "Interview."

75. Mikael Wood. "Katy Perry: *Teenage Dream*." *Spin*. www.spin
.com/reviews/katy-perry-teenage-dream-capitol.

76. Tony Sclafani. "Sex! Nudity! Why Katy Perry Is Hot." *Today Music*, August 27, 2010. http://today.msnbc.msn.com/id/38789777/ns/today-entertainment.

77. Quoted in Jocelyn Vena. "Katy Perry Responds to Rumors of Parents' Criticism: 'They Love and Support Me.'" MTV.com, August 20, 2008. www.mtv.com/news/articles/1593166/20080820/id_1962774.jhtml.

78. Quoted in Hollie McKay. "Pop Tarts: Christian Controversy; Katy Perry's Pastor Parents Upset She 'Kissed a Girl'?." FoxNews.com, July 25, 2008. www.foxnews.com/story/0,2933,391048,00.html.

79. Mike Rimmer. "Katy Perry: A Rare Interview with the Pop Star from her Christian Music Phase." Cross Rhythms, June 21, 2009. www.crossrhythms.co.uk/articles/music/Katy_Perry_A_rare_interview_with_the_pop_star_from_her_Christian_music_phase/36193/p1.

80. Quoted in Greenblatt. "'Girl' on Top."

81. Quoted in George Stephanopoulos. "Elmo to Katy Perry: 'We'll Have Another Play Date.'" ABCNews.com, September 24, 2010. http://blogs.abcnews.com/george/2010/09/elmo-to-katy-perry-well-have-another-play-date.html.

Chapter 6: Better than a Teenage Dream

82. Quoted in Carissa Rosenberg Tozzi. "Katy Perry." *Seventeen,* September 2010, p. 193.

83. Quoted in Tozzi. "Katy Perry." p. 183.

84. Quoted in Alison Prato. "Katy Perry Head over Heels." *Cosmopolitan,* November 2010, p. 38.

85. Quoted on ABC. *The View.* October 13, 2010. http://theview.abc.go.com/recap/wednesday-october-13-2010.

86. Katy Perry. TWIT BREAK. Twitter, October 19, 2010. http://twitter.com/katyperry/status/27868155212.

87. Quoted in CBSNews.com. "Katy Perry: Being a Pop Star Was My Plan." November 29, 2010. www.cbsnews.com/stories/2010/11/29/earlyshow/leisure/main7098940.shtml?tag=mncol;lst;2.

88. Quoted in James Montgomery. "Katy Perry Says She Wasn't Allowed to Watch 'The Smurfs' Growing Up." MTV.com, June 7, 2010. www.mtv.com/news/articles/1640953/katy-perry-wasnt-allowed-watch-smurfs-growing-up.jhtml.

89. Quoted in Megan Vick. "Katy Perry Gets Raunchy on 'The Simpsons.'" Billboard.com, December 6, 2010. http://www.billboard.com/column/viralvideos/katy-perry-gets-raunchy-on-the-simpsons-1004133756.story.

1984

Katy Hudson is born on October 25 in Santa Barbara, California.

1993

Begins singing in her church choir.

1997

Shows a strong talent for music and receives her first guitar as a birthday gift.

1999

Determined to pursue a career in music, she drops out of high school and passes the General Educational Development test.

2000

Catches the attention of a group of musicians in Nashville, who agree to work with her and help her enter the music business.

2001

Red Hill Records releases her first CD, titled *Katy Hudson*. The company goes bankrupt at the end of the year.

2002

Auditions for Glen Ballard, who then invites her to move to Los Angeles and try to launch her music career.

2003–2004

To avoid being confused with actress Kate Hudson, changes her last name to Perry.

2004

Production team The Matrix invites her to be lead singer for a new group they are forming; only weeks before the CD's release, the project is canceled.

2005

Prepares to release a new CD with Island Def Jam Music Group, but the company cancels the project; goes to work on a solo album for Columbia Records; records videos for "Diamonds" and for "Simple," which is picked up for the movie soundtrack and CD for the film *The Sisterhood of the Traveling Pants*.

2006
Columbia Records cancels her CD; provides background vocals and makes a video appearance in the single "Goodbye for Now" on the album *Testify* by P.O.D.; appears in videos for the songs "Cupid's Chokehold" by Gym Class Heroes and "Learn to Fly" by Carbon Leaf.

2007
Chris Anokute of Capitol Records convinces his company to sign Perry to a new contract; late in the year, "UR So Gay" is released as a single for download.

2008
Provides vocals and a video appearance in the single "Starstrukk" for the album *Want* by 3OH!3; travels with the Warped Tour; Capitol Records launches her CD *One of the Boys*, which lands on *Billboard* magazine's Top 200 chart at number nine; sings "I Kissed a Girl" on *So You Think You Can Dance*; records videos for "Hot n Cold," "I Kissed a Girl," and "Waking Up in Vegas"; her song "Fingerprints" is picked up for the movie *Baby Mama*; appears as herself on the television show *Wildfire*, singing in a nightclub; is featured on *The Young and the Restless*, portraying herself in a photo shoot.

2009
Capitol Records releases the CD *Katy Perry: MTV Unplugged*; adds vocals and a video appearance to the single "If We Ever Meet Again" for the album *Shock Value II* by Timbaland; her song "Hot n Cold" is added to the movies *The Proposal* and *The Ugly Truth*; "Hot n Cold" is sung by the Chipettes in the movie *Alvin and the Chipmunks: The Squeakquel*; meets comedian Russell Brand while filming a cameo for the movie *Get Him to the Greek*, and on New Year's Eve, the couple becomes engaged.

2010

Perry's CD recorded with group The Matrix is revived and released as *The Matrix* by Let's Hear It Records; records videos for the songs "California Gurls," "Firework," and "Teenage Dream"; Capitol Records releases her CD *Teenage Dream*; the movie *When in Rome* picks up Perry's song "If You Can Afford Me" as well as "Starstrukk"; appears in the movie video for *When in Rome* performing "Starstrukk" with 3OH!3; appears as herself in an episode of *Sesame Street* singing "Hot n Cold" with Elmo the Muppet, and the segment is suspended after complaints from parents that her outfit is too revealing; kicks off the new season of *Saturday Night Live* by singing "California Gurls" and "Teenage Dream" and also appears in a segment of "Bronx Beat"; marries Russell Brand at a private ceremony in India; performs at the American Music Awards and the Victoria's Secret Fashion Show; her new line of perfume, Kitty Purry, is launched; nominated for four Grammy Awards and appears on *The Simpsons*; "California Gurls" is ranked as the most-downloaded single in 2010 with 4.4 million downloads.

2011

Embarks on her world tour, *California Dreams*; is featured in the movie *The Smurfs* as the voice of Smurfette; sales of *Teenage Dream* reach 1 million copies, earning Perry a Platinum album award.

Books

Willia Baiotto, ed. *The Katy Perry Handbook—Everything You Need to Know About Katy Perry*. London: Tebbo, 2010. The ultimate resource for Katy Perry fans offers extensive references and links, photos, and information about her early life, career, personal life, music, filmography, and much more.

Dave Stone. *Russell Brand & Katy Perry: The Love Story*. London: John Blake, 2010. A detailed account of the life of Russell Brand and anecdotes about Katy Perry covering the time period from their initial meeting through their engagement.

Periodicals

"Find Out What Influences Katy Perry's Cute Style!." *Seventeen*, February 5, 2009.

Gary Graff. "Interview: Katy Perry—Hot n Bold." *Scotsman* (Edinburgh), February 21, 2009.

Leah Greenblatt. "'Girl' on Top." *Entertainment Weekly*, July 25, 2008.

Cortney Harding. "Single Lady." *Billboard*, January 31, 2009.

"Sex, God, and Katy Perry." *Rolling Stone*, August 19, 2010.

Rob Sheffield. "Girl on Girl: Katy Perry." *Blender*, September 24, 2008.

Rob Sheffield. "Katy Perry *Teenage Dream*." *Rolling Stone*, August 23, 2010.

Amy Spencer. "Katy Perry (She Kisses Boys, Too!)." *Glamour*, January 1, 2010.

Carissa Rosenberg Tozzi. "Katy Perry." *Seventeen*, September 2010.

Internet Sources

Stacey Anderson. "Katy Perry *One of the Boys*." *Spin*. www.spin.com/reviews/katy-perry-one-boys-capitol.

Jan Blumentrath. "Interview with Chris Anokute." Hit Quarters, October 18, 2010. www.hitquarters.com/index.php3?page=intrview/opar/intrview_Chris_Anokute_Interview.html.

Jennifer Boyer. "Katy Perry Holds Her Own on Warped Tour." Dead Hub, August 12, 2008. http://thedeadhub.com/2008/08/12/katy-perry-holds-her-own-on-warped-tour.

Russ Breimeier. "Katy Hudson." Review. *Christianity Today*. www.christianitytoday.com/ct/music/reviews/2001/katyhudson.html

Mike Burr. "Bathing Suits, Guyliner, and Mercury Worship." *Prefix*, February 6, 2008. www.prefixmag.com/features/katy-perry/interview/17027.

CBS News Entertainment. "'All Access': Katy Perry." February 4, 2009. www.cbsnews.com/stories/2009/02/04/entertainment/grammy2009/main4775775.shtml.

Lizzie Ennever. "Katy Perry *One of the Boys* Review." BBC Music, September 22, 2008. www.bbc.co.uk/music/reviews/dv25.

Alice Fisher. "So Much More than the Girl Next Door." *Observer* (London), June 14, 2009. www.guardian.co.uk/music/2009/jun/14/katy-perry-shepherds-bush-review?INTCMP=SRCH.

Christina Fuoco-Karasinski. "Perseverance Paying Off for Katy Perry." Live Daily, June 13, 2008. www.livedaily.com/archive/news/14375.html.

Jeff Giles. "Katy Perry: *One of the Boys.*" Bullz-Eye.com. www.bullz-eye.com/cdreviews/giles/katy_perry-one_of_the_boys.htm.

Darren Harvey. "Katy Perry—*One of the Boys.*" MusicOMH, September 15, 2008. www.musicomh.com/albums/katy-perry_0808.htm.

Genevieve Koski. "*One of the Boys.*" Onion, July 7, 2008. www.avclub.com/articles/katy-perry-one-of-the-boys,6983.

Patrick Luce. "Katy Perry Joins the Vans Warped Tour This Summer." Monsters and Critics, May 29, 2008. www.monstersandcritics.com/music/news/article_1408263.php/Katy_Perry_joins_The_Vans_Warped_Tour_this_summer.

James Montgomery. "Katy Perry Dishes on Her 'Long and Winding Road' from Singing Gospel to Kissing Girls." MTV News, June

24, 2008. www.mtv.com/news/articles/1589848/20080623/ id_1962774.jhtml.

James Montgomery. "Katy Perry Says She Wasn't Allowed to Watch 'The Smurfs' Growing Up." MTV.com, June 7, 2010. www.mtv.com/news/articles/1640953/katy-perry-wasnt-allowed-watch-smurfs-growing-up.jhtml.

Sunday Star Times (Fairfax, New Zealand). "Katy Perry: Girl Trouble." October 24, 2008. www.stuff.co.nz/sunday-star-times/entertainment/more-entertainment-stories/688815.

Christy Vowels. "Warped Tour in Cincinnati, Ohio: Cold Reception for Katy Perry." Associated Content, August 26, 2008. www.associatedcontent.com/article/958849/warped_tour_in_cincinnati_ohio_cold.html?cat=33.

Jon Wilde. "I'm a Natural-Born Glamour Ninja—and I Like It: Katy Perry on Her Unique Style." *Mail Online*, July 21, 2009. www.dailymail.co.uk/home/moslive/article-1198292/Im-natural-born-glamour-ninja--I-like-Katy-Perry.html.

Mikael Wood. "Katy Perry: *Teenage Dream*." *Spin*. www.spin .com/reviews/katy-perry-teenage-dream-capitol.

Websites

Katy Perry—Official Website (www.katyperry.com). This website maintained by Katy Perry includes photos, videos, news, schedules, merchandise, and links to social networking sites.

Katy Perry Source (http://katy-perry.us). A nonprofit unofficial fan site that features news, photos, and schedules of Perry's appearances.

"Katy Perry's Amazing Style Transformation," *Seventeen* (www .seventeen.com/fashion/makeovers/katy-perry-fashion-make over). A slide show of Perry's fashions from 2003 through 2009.

P.O.D. (band), 33

R
Recording Industry Association
   of America (RIAA), 31
Red Hill Records, 20
Reese, Dennis, 34

S
Sesame Street (TV program),
   79–80
"Simple" (song), 27, 28
The Simpsons (TV program), 93
Singh, Hanut, 84, 86
*The Sisterhood of the Traveling
   Pants* (film), 28, *29*
The Smurfs (film), 91
Snoop Dogg, *60*, 60–61
Spock, Scott, 27
Stefani, Gwen, 6, 46, *46*

T
Teen Choice Awards, 90
Teenage Dream (album), 62, 63
   controversy over, 72–74
"Teenage Dream" (song), 59, 72

video for, 73–74

U
Ultimate Woman of the Year
   Awards, 90
"UR So Gay" (song), 34, 50,
   68–69
USO Presents concert, 65, *66*,
   67

V
Vans Warped Tour, 44–45,
   47–48
Victoria's Secret Fashion
   Show, *92*

W
"Waking Up in Vegas" (song),
   71, 91
Wildfire (TV program), 44
Wilson Phillips, 21
Woodard, Cory, 65

Y
The Young and the Restless (TV
   program), 44

Anne K. Brown had difficulty choosing a career because she was interested in too many subjects. Finding her way into a career as an author and editor meant that she could continually explore new topics.

Brown has a degree in communication from the University of Wisconsin–Milwaukee. In the past, she has worked on fantasy role-playing games, fantasy fiction, magazine articles, and many different nonfiction topics. She is also an active Girl Scout and forensics coach. Brown lives in the Milwaukee area with her husband, two daughters, a black cat that is afraid of everything, and a collection of vintage Nancy Drew books.